Swapna Liddle's abiding love for the history of Delhi has translated into a PhD as well as several books and articles. She also seeks to raise awareness about the city's historic precincts through her work for the Indian National Trust for Art and Cultural Heritage (INTACH). She has written *Delhi: 14 Historic Walks*, *Chandni Chowk: The Mughal City of Old Delhi*, and has edited and annotated a translation of *Sair-ul-Manazil*.

ALSO BY SWAPNA LIDDLE

Delhi: 14 Historic Walks (2011)
Chandni Chowk: The Mughal City of Old Delhi (2017)

Connaught Place
and the Making of New Delhi

SWAPNA LIDDLE

SPEAKING TIGER PUBLISHING PVT. LTD
4281/4 Ansari Road, Daryaganj,
New Delhi—110002, India

First published in India in hardback by Speaking Tiger 2018

Copyright © Swapna Liddle 2018

ISBN: 978-93-88326-02-5
eISBN: 978-93-88326-01-8

10 9 8 7 6 5 4 3 2 1

Printed at:

All rights reserved.
No part of this publication may be reproduced, transmitted or stored
in a retrieval system, in any form or by any means,
electronic, mechanical, photocopying, recording or otherwise,
without the prior permission of the publisher.

This book is sold subject to the condition that it shall not, by
way of trade or otherwise, be lent, resold, hired out,
or otherwise circulated, without the publisher's
prior consent, in any form of binding or cover
other than that in which it is published.

Contents

	Acknowledgements	vi
	Introduction	ix
1.	The Idea of New Delhi	1
2.	A City is Planned	15
3.	Designing an Indian Capital	27
4.	New City on an Old Land	36
5.	The Garden City	48
6.	Building in Fits and Starts	64
8.	New Delhi Unveiled	81
9.	Connaught Place: Life of the City	99
10.	The Contours of Civic Life	113
11.	The Capital of Independent India	130
12.	The Changing Face of New Delhi and Connaught Place	141
	Notes	158
	List of Illustrations	175

Acknowledgements

MY INITIAL INVESTIGATION INTO HOW NEW DELHI came to be, was carried out in the context of an application to the United Nations Educational, Scientific and Cultural Organisation (UNESCO) for recognition of this twentieth-century capital, along with Shahjahanabad, the Mughal one, as a World Heritage Site. In the process I read extensively, attended illuminating lectures by experts and had numerous discussions with them. It is not possible to acknowledge all of them by name, but I would like to thank Mr A.G.K. Menon and Annabel Lopez, who directed the project for the Indian National Trust for Art and Cultural Heritage (INTACH), Delhi Chapter. It was long discussions with them that led to a development of my own thoughts on what makes New Delhi special.

This book, which is in many ways inspired by that project, owes its being to Renuka Chatterjee, who commissioned and edited it. Maithili Doshi and Neeti Banerji have worked diligently to give it it's beautiful final form. Gourab Banerji, as always, has used his language skills to 'settle' it. Sondeep Shankar, Jayshree Shukla, and Gopalan Rajamani generously shared their photographs. I am grateful to all of them.

I would also like to acknowledge all those who love the city of Delhi and its multi-layered history, and want to know more about it. It is your interest and concern that can ensure that this city's heritage will survive into the future.

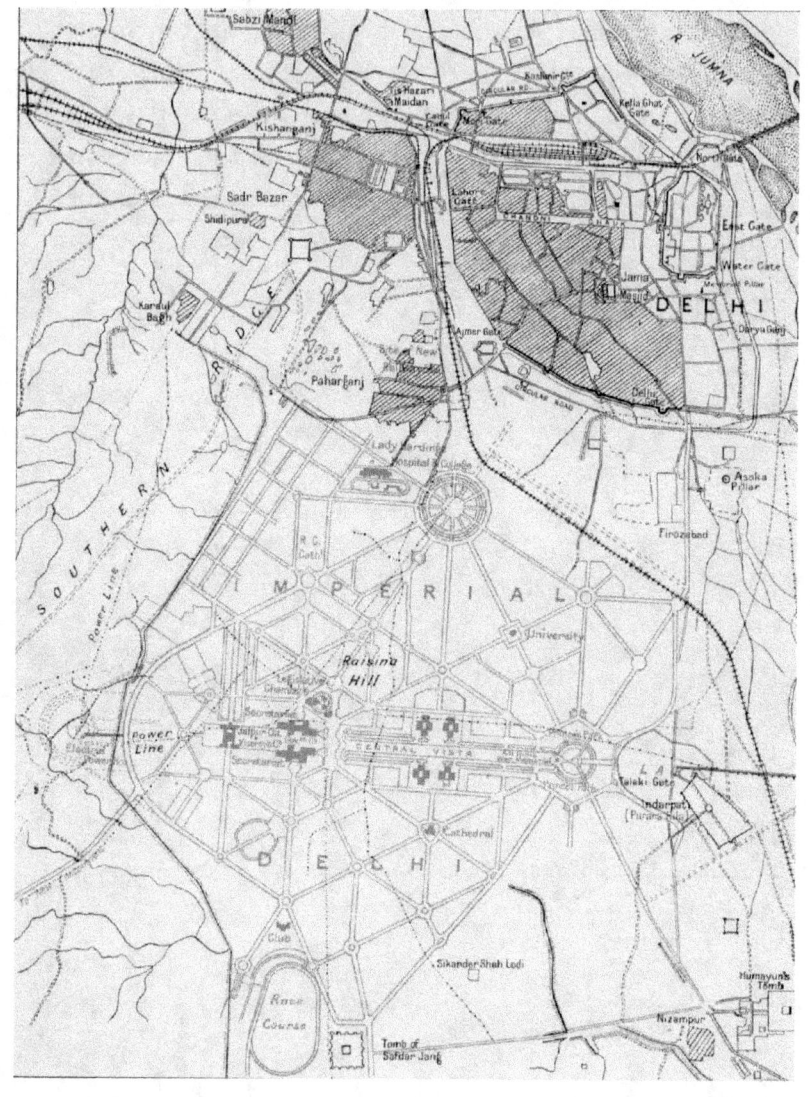

An outline of the city as planned

Introduction

NEW DELHI IS THE CAPITAL OF INDIA. IT IS ALSO ONE OF the largest cities in the world today. To those who know Delhi more closely, it is the alter ego of Old Delhi, which is the seventeenth-century Mughal city founded by Emperor Shahjahan. Few people know that 'New Delhi' was a name originally applied to a rather small part of the Delhi we know today. This was the core zone of the 'Imperial City', the capital of the British Raj, formally inaugurated in 1931. Roughly speaking, to the east it was bounded by Mathura Road and Purana Qila, to the west by the Central Ridge, and to the south by Safdarjung's Tomb and what we today know as Lodi Road. Its northern part was made up of a business and commercial district, which we know today as Connaught Place.

Things become clearer with the realization that what we today know as the metropolis of New Delhi, has grown out of a relatively modestly sized urban settlement, founded in the early twentieth century to serve as the new capital of British India. This city was the last in line of the several historic cities of Delhi, and has lent its name to the metropolis that has since grown around it.

This book is about the making of the city of New Delhi, and of Connaught Place, its iconic shopping, dining and recreational centre. It picks up the story at the beginning, when the idea of shifting the capital from Calcutta to Delhi first germinated in the minds of the British colonial rulers of India. It examines the process through which it was planned and built, and the people who played important roles in determining the shape it took. It looks at the social life that characterized it as the capital of one of the largest empires of all time, and its eventual transformation, as the capital of independent India.

My interest in New Delhi is part of my wider engagement with historic Delhi, its fascinating past, the impact of its rich heritage today, and its prospects in the future. Among all of Delhi's historic neighbourhoods, New Delhi probably faces the greatest challenge. Many question the continued existence and use of its major buildings and landmarks, on the ground that this is a colonial legacy that is perhaps better wiped out. Others feel that this expansive garden city reeks of elitism, and should be redeveloped on a denser plan.

I first set out to examine New Delhi's architectural and historic significance in some detail as part of a project undertaken by the Delhi Chapter of INTACH. This was the preparation of a dossier, applying to UNESCO for recognition of two cities of Delhi—Shahjahanabad and New Delhi, for World Heritage City status. Though the UNESCO recognition did not materialize, the research I did gave me valuable insights into what makes New Delhi special. I found that many of the conventional wisdoms about New Delhi needed to be challenged. There was something beyond the usual narrative of the arrogance of an empire wishing to leave its stamp on posterity, much as the Roman empire did, through its monumental architecture. At the level of smaller details, certain misconceptions, such as the credit given to Lutyens, by way of the name 'Lutyens' Delhi', were dispelled.

It is not that studies have not been done on New Delhi. The story of its historical background and significance, its planning and architecture, has been told through architectural and town planning studies, coffee table books, biographies of its architects, memoirs and historical monographs. Still, there is room for a concise, easy to read book, that will bring the available research together in an accessible form. I have tried to write just such a book. I have relied on published research of others, as well my own research, to put together an account of how New Delhi came to be. I hope that this will be adequately detailed for those who may not have read other, more scholarly, books on the subject, laying out the basic information. For those who have read other works, I trust that they will find new nuggets of information to make this one refreshing. My inclusion of endnotes will enable interested readers to follow the research further on their own if they wish.

SWAPNA LIDDLE
New Delhi, September 2018

The Government House, Calcutta; a painting by James Baillie Fraser, 1810s

The Idea of New Delhi

THE STORY OF NEW DELHI IS USUALLY TRACED TO A moment in December 1911, at the Coronation Durbar then being held in Delhi. The Durbar, a grand assemblage held to celebrate the coronation of George V as the Emperor of India, was a tradition inspired by Mughal durbars. The British had adapted this tradition with a view to inspiring loyalty and attachment in their Indian subjects, by using a symbolic language that was familiar to them. Similar events had been held at Delhi to commemorate the assumption of the imperial title by the two previous British monarchs—Victoria in 1877 and Edward VII in 1903. The Durbar of 1911 was not only on a larger scale than these previous events, it was also the first occasion that the monarch himself was attending.

The main Durbar event, held on 12 December, was the formal assemblage of a large number of officials and dignitaries, including rulers of semi-independent Indian states who were under the sovereign authority of the British Crown. In his closing speech the Emperor dropped a bombshell: 'We are pleased to announce to Our People...We have decided upon the transfer of the seat of the Government of India from Calcutta to the ancient Capital of Delhi, and simultaneously, as a consequence of that transfer, the creation at as early a date as possible of a Governorship for the Presidency of Bengal... It is Our earnest desire that these changes may conduce to the better administration of India, and the greater prosperity and happiness of our beloved people.' As a corollary, three days later two 'foundation stones' were laid at the vast Durbar site itself, marking the intention to build a new city to house the imperial capital.

The announcement was initially greeted by astonishment all round, since it was so unexpected for the vast majority who heard it. The surprise was soon followed by both positive and negative responses. The superstitious among the naysayers saw an omen of 'great danger to the British Raj' in an accident that occurred the day after the announcement. This was when a ship named *Delhi*, belonging to the Peninsular & Oriental Line, carrying the King's sister, Princess Louise, and her husband, the Duke of Fife, was wrecked in the Straits of Gibraltar in heavy seas; though they fortunately escaped unharmed. The foundation stone laying ceremony also became involved in some controversy. A simple set of stones that had been prepared by the Public Works Department were used, and a rumour began to circulate that tombstones had been repurposed due to the need to rush the work.

The laying of the foundation stones marked the beginning of the planning process, which would see the city take shape over the next two decades. It also marked the culmination of a well-thought-out policy decision, though one that had been debated within a very small circle. From the earliest days of the East India Company's growing control over the subcontinent, even as early as 1782, the idea of a capital other than Calcutta had been discussed. The reasons generally put forward were strategic and operational, as Calcutta was tucked away on the eastern coast, at a great distance from many of the far-flung provinces of the growing empire of

The laying of the foundation stones of New Delhi; a photograph from the official album of the Durbar

the British in India. The idea never went any further, and by the mid-nineteenth century, with the growth of a network of communication and transport—particularly the railways, the relatively remote location of Calcutta was no longer of great relevance.

When the question of an alternative capital was raised again in 1911, it was in the context of a very changed political situation. The national movement was growing, and Indians were becoming vocal in their criticism of British rule. The government, under the viceroyalty of Lord Curzon (1899-1905), initially sought to weaken the movement through the divisive measure of partitioning Bengal. Though purportedly an administrative measure required for better governance of the large and unwieldy province, the motive behind it was to divide the large Bengali-speaking population along communal lines. The move resulted in an upsurge of popular protest, and the rise of episodes of revolutionary violence, both of which soon spread far beyond the borders of Bengal.

The failure of the partition to curb the national movement led Curzon's successors, Lord Minto (1895-1910) and Lord Hardinge (1910-16), to embark on a different course—that of political reform. The Indian Councils Act of 1909, popularly known as the Morley-Minto reforms (after the Viceroy and the Secretary of State responsible for them) for the first time introduced a limited elected membership in the legislative councils in the centre and the provinces. There was also a strong feeling, growing among officials, that the partition of Bengal along communal lines had been a mistake, and ought to be revoked. It was these political imperatives which lead in a logical progression to the decision not only to transfer the capital, but to transfer it to Delhi.

The initial deliberations took place between the Viceroy, Hardinge, and the Finance and Home Members of his Council—Guy Fleetwood Wilson and John Lewis Jenkins, respectively. Their suggestions took the form of an official report, titled *Transfer of the Seat of Government from Calcutta to Delhi and the Constitutional Changes in Bengal*. Drafted by Jenkins, its third paragraph read: 'It is certain that, in the course of time, the just demands of Indians for a larger share in the Government of the country will have to be satisfied, and the question will be how this devolution of power can be conceded without impairing the supreme authority of the Governor General in Council. The only possible solution of the difficulty would be gradually giving the provinces a larger measure of self-government until at last, India would consist of a number of administrations, autonomous in all provincial affairs, with the Government of India above them all and possessing power to interfere in cases of misgovernment, but ordinarily restricting their functions to matters of imperial concern.'

The idea of greater devolution of power had been developing for quite some time before the proposals for the holding of a durbar and of a transfer of capital were officially considered. Wilson had written in his diary in 1910, 'It is but human to prefer reasonably good government administered by one's own race rather than extreme efficiency at the hands of an alien race.' He also subscribed to the belief that educated and intelligent Indians desired not independence but self-government, so that India 'may take her place in the empire not as a mere dependency but on terms of equality and coordination.' Wilson went further than any of his colleagues in contemplating the future of Indian political development, saying, 'British India is not yet ripe for self-government, but if all goes well it very soon will be.'

Many have seen the creation of New Delhi as the articulation of imperial authority—an essentially conservative, even regressive idea. A closer look at the official correspondence suggests that it was an altogether different kind of empire that was being envisaged, which saw a greater devolution of power to the provinces, and by implication a system that was more responsive to local Indian needs. Not only was the partition of Bengal being modified along more acceptable lines, Bengal was now to be formed into a full-fledged province. The transfer of the capital was a crucial part of the reform, because, in order for devolution to be meaningful, it was imperative that the provinces be given breathing room, and the capital not be too closely associated with any one province.

Many years later, after the new capital had been inaugurated, one of its prominent officials (John Thompson, Chief Commissioner, Delhi, 1928-32) would look back at Hardinge's proposal to the Secretary of State in these words: 'The move to Delhi was indeed a preparation for a future different from the past. Hardinge's dispatch looked forward to a day when India would consist of a number of administrations, autonomous in all provincial affairs.'

Once the proposal was made public, reactions to it

started pouring in. The very fact that it stood for reform and devolution made the transfer unacceptable to its critics in official circles. The most vocal among these, Curzon, said in a speech in the House of Lords: 'My fear about this establishment of the capital at Delhi is that...as the Provinces follow the line you have laid down and demand increasing Home Rule, your viceroy in Delhi will become a sort of puppet as the Moguls were towards the end of their regime, and India will break up into separate fragments, as it did in the expiring days of Aurangzeb and his successors.' Critics also felt that the reversal of the partition would be an acknowledgement of weakness on the part of the colonial state, and encourage Indians to think that persistent agitation would always yield results.

On the other side of the divide, the Indian nationalist leaders, too, saw the transfer for what it promised. Gopal Krishna Gokhale viewed the announcement in Delhi as a commitment not only by the Government of India, but by the Emperor himself, to a 'policy of autonomy for the different provinces.' One of the chief defenders of the transfer, Edwin Montagu, Undersecretary of State for India, acknowledged that the change was a recognition of Indian nationalist sentiment, which could not be turned back through repressive policies such as the partition of Bengal. Instead, political reforms could turn these energies in a positive direction, leading to a meeting of cultures 'not with clash or discord but in harmony and amity' and 'as a great Bengali writer [Rabindranath Tagore] has laid it down, the East and West must meet at the "altar of humanity".'

Hardinge, from the official Durbar album

Despite articulations of this sort, one must realize that these political changes were not the result of any great idealism or magnanimity on the part of British policy-makers, or sympathy with the Indians people's right to self-governance. They were a pragmatic response to a situation where all other practical means of dealing with the national movement seemed to have failed, as evidenced by the reactions to the partition of Bengal. In a speech of 1913, Wilson spoke of the dawn of a new era in India, in which 'we shall have to resort to the more difficult arts of persuasion and conciliation, in the place of the easier methods of autocracy.' In that sense, the idea of a new capital was, in the words of Jenkins, 'a bold stroke of statesmanship', because it sought to secure the ends of empire through new means— through the consent of educated Indians who had begun to agitate for independence. Devolution was seen as a way of safeguarding the future of British rule in India. These concessions had actually been wrested by Indians through a long period of nationalist struggle, particularly by the Congress movement since the 1880s.

Once the need for a new capital had been accepted, from there to the choice of Delhi was not too big a leap. There were practical reasons that made Delhi a good choice for the capital of the British Indian empire. Its advantages of location included equidistance from the major commercial centres of Calcutta and Bombay, and closer proximity to Simla. The latter was important because the upper echelons of government used to make an annual migration to Simla, where they spent the summer months. The climate of Delhi

The Mughal capital of Shahjahanabad; a painting by Charles Stewart Hardinge, 1840s

was in fact better than Calcutta, and a longer winter meant that the sojourn in Simla would not need to be as long. Delhi was also easily accessible from different parts of the country, located at the junction of six railway lines. Finally, located in North India, it was closer to the majority of the princely states.

But far greater than these pragmatic considerations, was the symbolic importance of Delhi. If an overarching imperial structure was to be the future of the British Raj, no better capital could be found than Delhi—the seat of the great erstwhile empires of India. Since the early thirteenth century it had functioned, with a few interregnums, as a capital of important powers—the Delhi Sultanate and the Mughal Empire. The memory of those times was strong. In 1905-06, the Prince of Wales, who would later become George V, visited India. During that visit, he was to later recall, the Regent of Jodhpur, Partab Singh, mentioned that a capital at Delhi would be desirable, 'as being in every way more convenient and on account of its historical associations with the ancient Government of India.' Hardinge himself was very aware of popular opinion in India. He wrote, 'Delhi is still a name to conjure with. It is intimately associated in the minds of the Hindus with sacred legends which go back even beyond the dawn of history...To the Mohammedans it would be a source of unbounded gratification to see the ancient capital of the Moguls restored to its proud position as the seat of the Empire.'

Lord Crewe, Secretary of State for India, responded positively to the Government of India's proposal, and the choice of Delhi. He wrote, 'not only do the ancient walls of Delhi enshrine an Imperial tradition comparable with that of Constantinople, or with that of Rome itself, but the near neighbourhoods of the existing city formed the theatre for some most notable scenes in the old-time drama of Hindu history, celebrated in the vast treasure house of national epic verse.'

Both Hardinge and Crewe, in keeping with the prevalent colonial understanding of their time, saw Indian society and its history as being divided rigidly along religious lines. To them the Mughal empire was a Muslim one, towards which only Muslims could look with any nostalgia. This, of course, was not true. Till well into the nineteenth century, Hindu as well as Muslim rulers of princely states continued to pay homage to the Mughal emperor. In 1857, Hindus as well as Muslim soldiers, princes and peasants had rallied behind the Mughal emperor to rise up against the British.

Hardinge, however, was right in saying that the site of Delhi had associations that went back into ancient history, and past it into the realm of myth and legend. Delhi's old name was Indraprastha, a name that came from the Hindu god Indra, who was believed to have performed ritual sacrifices on the banks of the Yamuna at this site. People also believed that the site of the Purana Qila, where the Mughal Emperor Humayun built a fort in the sixteenth century, marked the location of the city built by the Pandavas, the heroes of the epic, the *Mahabharata*. British official pronouncements were eager to underline these associations. To those invited to the foundation stone laying ceremony on 15 December 1911, the invitations sent out described the event as 'inaugurating the *restoration of Delhi as the Capital of India* by laying foundation-stones' [emphasis mine].

Significant non-official opposition to the transfer of the capital came mainly from Calcutta, and, in particular, from the commercial interests that were concentrated in the city that had been the centre of British India for over a century. The Bengal Chamber of Commerce, and various bodies representative of the European population of Calcutta expressed their disapproval. Criticism was also voiced in the press—newspapers such as the *Statesman*, the *Pioneer* and the *Amrita Bazar Patrika* decried the move. Heated debates on the subject also took place in the British Houses of Parliament, where the Liberal government was subjected to sharp criticism from the Conservative opposition.

The critics dwelt on a number of other points. They deplored the fact that the decision had been taken in secrecy without consulting the Legislative Council, or even the Lieutenant Governors and Governors of the provinces. The suitability of Delhi as a site for the capital was questioned. It was said that the climate was not healthy, it caused fevers and boils. It was a lifeless backwater of the Punjab province, remote from the major centres of commerce—Calcutta, Bombay, Karachi, and therefore the capital and the officials would end up in a bureaucratic enclave, distant from important public opinion. Even the symbolic importance of Delhi's heritage was questioned—was it not, as one newspaper put it, a graveyard of dynasties?

Among the various arguable weaknesses of the plan, the issue of the financial outlay was the most obvious and easy target of attack. The debate over the financing of the capital also ultimately came down to a question of the basic understanding of the future role of the empire. Was British rule in India to serve the business interests of the British, or of their colonial subjects, and in what proportion? Those who stood for the continuation of Calcutta as the capital, supported the continuation of the old system of Empire, exclusively by and for British interests. In the words of Curzon, Calcutta was the 'expression of British rule in India, it is English built, English commerce has made it the second city in the empire...English statesmen, administrators, and generals have built up to its present commanding height the fabric of British rule in India.' This was at sharp variance with any opinion that aimed at giving Indians a more participatory role in the empire.

The foundation of the city of New Delhi was thus mired in controversies, around the very nature of colonial rule and of the British Indian empire. In retrospect, one could probably say that the path to New Delhi as the capital of independent India, finally achieved in 1947, was being laid, though the protagonists at the time could not grasp its significance.

Purana Qila; a painting by Thomas Daniell, 1790s

A City is Planned

THE ESSENTIAL WISDOM OF TRANSFERRING THE CAPITAL FROM Calcutta to Delhi continued to be debated in the press, in official and non-official circles, and in the British Parliament through 1912. In the meanwhile, steps were being taken to put the plan into action. Hardly had the announcement of the transfer been made, that ideas about how the new city would be planned began to be talked about.

Hardinge was acutely aware of the importance of planning the new city well, and was determined not to hand over the task to the Public Works Department. Instead, he wanted a 'small but strong, Committee to deal with planning, building and organization of the new Delhi.' This committee was concerned primarily with the general layout, while the architectural design of the actual buildings would come later. As to the composition of the committee, two names were settled on fairly quickly. One was that of John A. Brodie, a municipal engineer from Liverpool. The other was George Swinton, the chairman of the London County Council, the foremost municipal body in Britain. He had also spent several years in India, and therefore, had some experience of the country.

It took a little longer to decide the third name, that of an architect-cum-town planner. Three names were suggested. One was that of Herbert Baker, who had designed the government buildings at Pretoria, the capital of South Africa. Another was that of Henry Vaughan Lanchester, who had recently been engaged by Maharaja Scindia to advise on the improvement of a part of Gwalior town. The third name was that of Edwin Landseer Lutyens, an architect with a background mainly in building expensive homes. He was very highly thought of by those who were familiar with his work, one of his admirers suggesting that he 'be the moving genius from the outset…An exceptional man is best, and Lutyens is a very exceptional man.' Hardinge was initially not convinced, saying, 'My fear about him is that he is more of a country-house architect and has no experience of anything big.' Crewe, however, swung the opinion in favour of Lutyens, and he was picked. The committee was engaged for a term of five months. Lanchester was engaged for a period of one month as an additional consulting expert.

The Town Planning Committee's immediate task was to settle on an appropriate site for the future capital. In an audience with the British monarch just before their departure for India, the members of the committee had been told to keep an open mind, and not consider themselves bound to the site where the foundation stones had been laid. The question of a suitable site had also started being discussed in India almost immediately after the transfer of the capital had been made public. Though the foundation stones had been laid at the site of the Durbar, those familiar with Delhi were aware of one major drawback of the area—a very high water table and the proneness to flooding. Hardinge had begun to explore various sites to the south of Shahjahanabad, and even before the arrival of the committee, had visited Malcha (at the foot of the Ridge, in the vicinity of today's Chanakyapuri) and Naraina, which lay to the southwest of Shahjahanabad.

Arriving in Delhi on 15 April 1912, the members of the Town Planning Committee stayed at the Maiden's Hotel, located in Civil Lines, and spent a very busy five weeks. Despite the increasing heat, they made several trips surveying the land around the city, and held meetings with local officials to assess the potentialities of various sites. Once their fieldwork in Delhi was over, on 20 May they fled the heat of Delhi to Simla, the summer capital, to hold a final round of discussions with officials in the pleasant weather of the hill station. On 13 June, the committee submitted its first report to the government, on the subject of a suitable site.

The team had visited and assessed a number of potential sites, and the pros and cons of each were discussed in the report. One alternative, which was briefly considered before being discarded, was that of the east bank of the Yamuna, across the river from Shahjahanabad. The major factor which ruled this out was that the river physically separated it from the existing city. This would not be practical, since it was envisaged that the majority of the population would continue to live in the old city. Another option was to the west of the Ridge—Naraina and its surroundings. While this was in many ways a suitable site, it was rejected on the ground that it 'could not be considered to be Delhi'. The problem was that the intervening Ridge not only cut off easy communication with the existing city, but obstructed 'all view of the older Delhis of the past'. Since Delhi had in the first place been chosen for its great symbolic significance as a capital of historic Indian empires, this was a significant drawback.

Another possible location was north of Shahjahanabad, which included the site of the Durbar, where the foundation stones had been laid. For many within British Indian officialdom, this was a popular choice. For those concerned with symbolism, this place was associated with the durbars celebrating the coronation of three British monarchs. Going back further, this location included the Ridge, which was associated with the Revolt of 1857, where the British forces had made their successful stand to retake Delhi and turn the tide of the countrywide revolt. For those who were economically minded, there was the thought that this site could be converted into a suitable capital with the least expense. It already contained a number of public buildings and bungalows—the 'Civil Lines', housing a mainly European business and administrative population.

Yet the Town Planning Committee rejected the site. They rejected it on the very ground that part of it was already built up, as they pointed out, in a haphazard fashion. There was no question of adding buildings to the pre-existing Civil Lines. This could hardly be a 'town-planning scheme worthy of an Imperial City'. On the other hand, purchasing the land and levelling all the construction on it to start afresh, would be too expensive. In any case, the Civil Lines area was just a small part of the whole site. The adjoining land, the vast plain where the durbars had been held, was prone to flooding. There were also important ideological reasons that made the Civil Lines and Durbar sites unsuitable for the new capital. These were areas which symbolized the old Raj, and its confrontation with the Indian people, most notably in 1857. If the new capital was to represent a reworked relationship, these old precedents would have to be de-emphasized.

By a process of elimination, the site that was settled upon by the committee was to the east of the Ridge, south of Shahjahanabad, between the village of Malcha (on the Ridge) and the sixteenth-century fortress known as Purana Qila. The location had much to recommend it. It was not very built up, though its southern and eastern edges contained the remains of many old tombs and other structures. Also importantly, an eminence in the middle of the site (Raisina Hill) commanded a view of all the cities of Delhi laid out beside the river. Looking eastward and starting from the left, one could see Shahjahanabad, fourteenth-century Ferozabad, Purana Qila, and further to the right, the tomb of the emperor Humayun and the Sufi shrine of Nizamuddin. This was a site that could connect the new capital to the imperial past of India.

An interesting subplot of this story was an alternate plan that the government briefly considered at the end of 1912. Drawn up by a railway engineer, Bradford Leslie, the builder of Howrah Bridge in Calcutta, the plan would put the capital back in the northern site. It proposed the construction of a weir across the Yamuna, which would lead to the creation of a lake, providing valuable lakefront property. Additional land would be reclaimed by building an embankment, alongside which would run a wide boulevard, lined with 'trees, shops, restaurants, theatres, clubs, hotels, and cafes'. The proposal was rejected on various grounds, mainly health and sanitation, since the damming of the Yamuna would increase the water table and intensify malarial conditions.

While the question of a site was being settled, the creation of a suitable town plan was also being thought out. Most of the ideas informing this tentative plan came from Lutyens, who wrote to his wife, 'it is my site, my layout, etc., so I am pleased'. Having made their submissions, the committee departed. Passing through Delhi on their way from Simla to Bombay, they met Lanchester there, and spent two days with him, going over the southern site and explaining the draft plan that they had made out. It was understood that Lanchester would concentrate mainly on the improvement of the old city of Shahjahanabad, and its better connection with the new capital. In passing, however, he made some comments on the committee's plan too.

Lanchester's intervention was to be a crucial one. Hardinge, examining the Town Planning Committee's scheme in the light of Lanchester's comments, began to see the weaknesses in it. A visit to Delhi at the end of July, to examine the plan on the ground, convinced him of the serious flaws in the proposed alignments. In a letter to Reginald Craddock (who had succeeded Jenkins as Home Member) he went so far as to remark, 'In my opinion there has been a singular lack of common sense in the plans of the Delhi Committee.' Craddock agreed with Hardinge, commenting, 'I think Lanchester is worth all the experts put together,' and suggesting that he be given a permanent assignment and the services of the committee dispensed with.

Though this was not done, and Lanchester had to be content with his one month in India, during that period he worked furiously, in consultation with Hardinge, to prepare a series of alternate plans. In the light of Lanchester's inputs, Hardinge rejected most of Lutyens' suggestions. One of the issues that had to be tackled was the alignment of the main avenue of the city (what we know today as Rajpath). Lutyens had designed this to lead from the Viceroy's residence (now Rashtrapati Bhavan), which was located at Malcha, to Jama Masjid. This avenue terminated at the southwest corner of the mosque, which was a blank wall at the rear, hardly a very pleasing prospect for the main street of the imperial city. In addition, in the path of this proposed avenue lay the populous settlement of Paharganj. The main axis of the new capital, as planned, would necessitate the clearing of this land. This would be not only an expensive proposition, as land prices were high, but a move that would be unpopular with its 35,000-odd inhabitants.

Lutyens' grid plan, too, was discarded, in favour of one which incorporated a mix of straight, curving and radial roads. His suggestion that the ceremonial avenue be lined with the palaces of the maharajas, with huge frontages and imposing gates, was also considered impractical. Among the committee's sins of omission had been their failure to take into account some important pre-existing religious structures—two Hindu temples fell in the path of the originally proposed central avenue, and the Idgah in the middle of one of the proposed roads. It was politically inexpedient to demolish these. In the reworked plan, not only were these preserved, but other existing monuments such as Humayun's Tomb and Safdarjung's Tomb were incorporated as terminal points of important avenues.

The back wall of the Jama Masjid

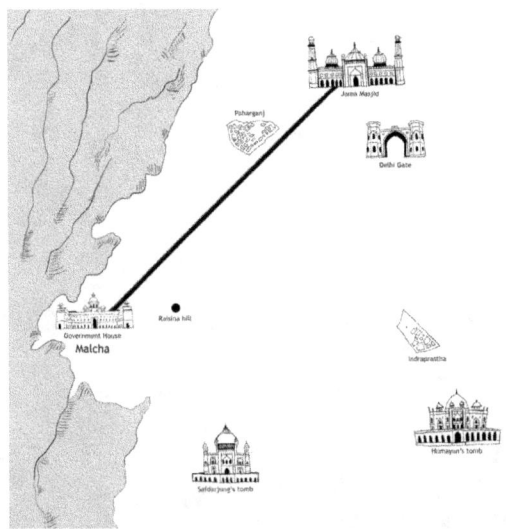

The location and orientation of Government House in the initial plan of the Town Planning Committee

Hardinge was himself responsible for one important decision—the precise orientation and location of the Viceroy's residence, or Government House. Lutyens' plan to have the house look down the ceremonial avenue to the back of Jama Masjid, was abandoned. Instead, the orientation of Government House and the ceremonial avenue was turned to squarely face Purana Qila, with a view of the Jama Masjid to the left, and Safdarjung's Tomb to the right, so that the 'view would comprise all the ancient monuments and objects of historic interest in one comprehensive panorama'. This was a principle on which Lanchester and Swinton agreed, though, as Swinton put it, 'Lutyens, of course, has little sympathy with these remains.'

The location of Government House at Malcha had

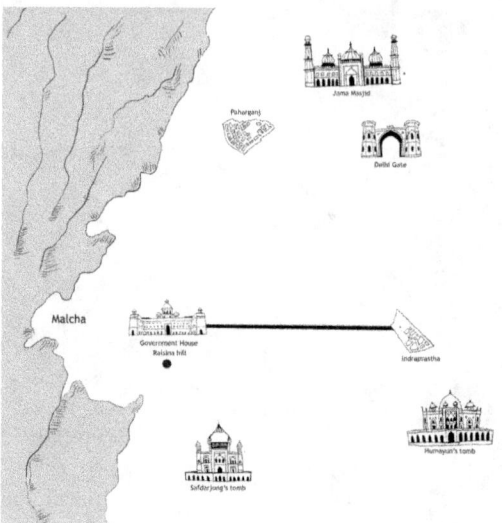

The final location and orientation of Government House

posed many problems. In the reworked plan it meant that the ceremonial avenue leading from Government House to Purana Qila would pass through a hundred-foot cut in Raisina Hill, which stood in the middle. This would cause a traffic bottleneck and in addition, the view of Government House up the vista would also be severely constricted. Eventually Hardinge accepted the suggestion, originally put forward by Brodie, to place Government House on Raisina hill itself. This solved another problem with Lutyens' avenue—its excessive length, which according to the original plan, would be some two miles.

It was left to the Town Planning Committee to further tweak this plan. In the layout they finally submitted, the focal point was the Government House located on Raisina Hill.

From here a broad avenue ran due east, to the northwestern gate of Purana Qila. Halfway down this avenue, on the level ground, lay the Secretariat buildings. Through this Secretariat area ran another avenue, intersecting with the main avenue at right angles. At the southern end of this second avenue, a cathedral was planned. At the northern end, the railway station would be constructed, surrounded by a circular arrangement of administrative and municipal offices, post office, shops and hotels. This was the future Connaught Place, eventually built with several modifications.

An interesting feature of the plan was the revival of the riverfront. Though several of Delhi's historic cities had been built on the banks of the Yamuna, over the past several decades the river had been changing its course eastwards. Lanchester, in his early comments, had suggested various means of integrating both the new and old cities better with the Yamuna. The committee's plan now was to bring the river back to its old course, and with its water, even create a lake in front of Purana Qila. A riverside drive would lead from Civil Lines to Purana Qila. The report also laid considerable emphasis on linking the new city with the older city of Shahjahanabad. This was to be done, firstly, through a widening of the road which led southwards from the Red Fort to Purana Qila; and secondly, by having one avenue lead from the area now known as Vijay Chowk, towards the Jama Masjid. Before it reached Jama Masjid, it would divide into two, one branch going towards Kashmiri Gate, and the other towards the southern, or Delhi gate of the Red Fort.

The committee made one final change before submitting its report in March 1913. The Secretariat buildings would now share the elevated position on Raisina Hill along with Government House. How this came to be, and what would be the consequences, is a story that will be told a little later. For now, the final report of the Committee was submitted to the Viceroy, after which the team departed for England again.

There was a postscript to the drastic reworking of the committee's preliminary plans by Lanchester and Hardinge, which revealed the intense rivalry between the two architects —Lutyens and Lanchester. In a letter to Swinton, Hardinge mentioned that he was annoyed because he had heard 'that Lanchester conveys the impression in England that he has succeeded in upsetting Lutyens' apple-cart...I wish people would not talk of apple-carts being upset. What does it matter who it may be who suggests a site or a plan, provided that we get the best? It is upon that we should concentrate, and not such petty puerilities as apple-carts.'

The evolution of the town plan of New Delhi, as outlined above, can be traced through the notes and correspondence of the principal players responsible. In particular, the roles of Lanchester and Hardinge were crucial in determining the fundamentals of the final scheme. Many of the suggestions of the Town Planning Committee, which came from the architect member, Lutyens, had been rejected. Yet, strangely, in the decades to come, Lanchester and Hardinge's contributions would be all but forgotten, and New Delhi would be popularly known as 'Lutyens' Delhi'.

Swinton Jacob's Indo-Saracenic St Stephen's College, 1891

Designing an Indian Capital

WHILE THE TOWN PLAN HAD BEEN TAKING SHAPE, THE question of the appointment of the main architects for the important public buildings, such as Government House and the Secretariats, was also being debated. Though initially the opinion in official circles was that commissions for an important project such as this should be through open competition, that idea was soon dropped. A suitable architect, or rather architects, since the project was deemed to be too large, therefore had to be chosen.

Lutyens, while still a member of the Town Planning Committee, had begun to work on some preliminary sketches for Government House, and was hopeful that he would get the entire commission. Hardinge, though impressed with his proposals, had doubts about Lutyens' suitability. At the root of the objection lay Lutyens' very negative view of Indian architecture, and his insistence on using a purely European style for the government buildings. The issue of architectural idiom was crucial. The earliest pronouncement on the importance of style had come from George V himself, in his speech at the laying of the foundation stones during the Durbar of 1911. He had said, 'It is my desire that the planning and designing of the public buildings to be erected will be considered with the greatest deliberation and care, so that the new creation may be in every way worthy of this ancient and beautiful city.'

So, what was worthy of a city that boasted of some of the grandest monumental architecture of Sultanate and Mughal times? The idea of a new capital at Delhi had been conceived as part of a new vision of governance for India, to give Indians a greater stake in the empire. For the important architects of that decision, George V and Hardinge, it was crucial that the very buildings of the new capital express that sentiment. They were, therefore, enthusiastic supporters of an Indian style. In a meeting with Lutyens in March 1912, the King had expressed himself as being in favour of the Mughal style. Hardinge agreed on the need for an Indian look for the new city, and reported that the rulers of the Indian princely states, Indian members of the Legislative Council, and in fact, Indian public opinion in general, was inclined in that direction.

The most coherent campaigner for the Indic style was

E.B. Havell, retired principal of the Calcutta School of Art. In a letter to the *Times* just ten days after the Durbar, he expressed the opinion that by shifting to Delhi, the government would 'leave the commercial atmosphere of Calcutta, with its shoddy imitations of European architecture...and find itself in the heart of Hindustan, where the artistic traditions of Indian building are still, for all practical architectural purposes, as much alive as they were when Akbar, by calling into the service of the State the skill of Hindu temple builders, gave Saracenic (i.e. Islamic) architecture in India a wonderful new impulse.'

Here, Havell was clearly addressing the ideological underpinnings of the transfer of the capital from Calcutta to Delhi. There was to be a departure from the old regime, which was too closely associated with the British commercial interests that Calcutta represented. The new Raj was an Indian empire, in the tradition of other great empires of Indian history. The example to follow was that of Akbar, the Mughal ruler, who through his policy of 'sulh-e-kul', had set the state above partisan interests, treating all subjects equally, irrespective of religious beliefs or ethnic differences. It was this impulse that had to be reflected in the architecture of the new city.

Hardinge, as the head of the government in India, was acutely alive to the political implications of the choice of architectural idiom. He induced Lutyens to visit Mandu, Indore, Lucknow and Kanpur in December 1912, to receive inspiration from the architecture to be found in these historic locations. Lutyens, however, was harshly critical when it

Herbert Baker *Edwin Lutyens*

came to evaluating the Indian architectural tradition, and could find no redeeming features in it at all. He was dismissive of Hardinge's ideological concerns, saying, 'I do want old England to stand up and plant her great traditions and good taste where she goes and not pander to sentiment and all this silly Moghul-Hindu stuff.'

Fortuitously, a letter appeared in the *Times* newspaper in London, on this very issue of a suitable style for the new imperial capital. It was written by Herbert Baker, whose name had been mentioned very early as a possible candidate for membership of the Town Planning Committee. This letter brought Baker again into the limelight, for he expressed views close in sentiment to the official line, remarking that, 'British rule in India is not a mere veneer of government and culture. It is a new civilization in growth, a blend of the best elements of East and West...It is to this great fact that the architecture of Delhi should bear testimony.' The government, which was looking for precisely this attitude, was gratefully welcoming. Swinton remarked: 'Here we have a man who is a successful architect and speaks not only like a poet, but like a statesman.'

By happy chance, Lutyens and Baker were personal friends, and admired each other's work. Soon, the idea that both might work together on the project, had gained currency. When it was conveyed to Lutyens that his candidature may be accepted if he agreed to the collaboration, he assented with alacrity, remarking, 'Baker has a delightful personality and most pleasant to work with.' Lutyens by now was also trying to appear more accommodating, according to Hardinge, 'quite ready to adopt Indian architectural details in any designs that might be confided to him.'

So, by mid-January 1913, a collaboration between Lutyens and Baker had been agreed on, with one condition. This was the appointment of Swinton Jacob as an associate, or an architectural adviser. Swinton Jacob was an architect with a long career in India. He was a practitioner of the Indo-Saracenic style, which sought to make modern buildings with emphatically Indian features, and had been a popular movement in India from the 1870s. Jacob himself had designed important buildings such as St Stephen's College at Kashmiri Gate in Delhi, Daly College in Indore, and the Canning and Medical Colleges in Lucknow. Hardinge hoped that Jacob would ensure that Indian features were used in New Delhi's architecture. It was only when Lutyens accepted this collaboration and agreed to adapting his designs to official requirements, that his commission was finalized.

Apart from the appointment of the architects, administrative and infrastructural details also had to be worked out before the city could begin to take shape. To begin with, on 1 October 1912, a special enclave of Delhi was created, covering an area of 557 square miles, and with a population of 392,000. It was put under a Chief Commissioner, Malcolm Hailey, who was also appointed the president of the Imperial Delhi Committee. This committee, which controlled the plan and execution of the New Delhi project, consisted of the president, an architect, an engineer and a finance officer, assisted by a secretary. Lutyens, Baker and Jacob were to constitute an 'architectural board', responsible for the design of the main government buildings, and also to advise on general matters of design in the city.

The site of New Delhi—view from Humayun's Tomb to Purana Qila

An important step in the process of city planning was acquisition of land, amounting to some 40,000 acres, that had been designated as the area required for the new city. In order to keep costs low, urban areas such as Paharganj, had been excluded. So, most of the area of the proposed capital was rural and agricultural. For the purposes of planning and acquisition the total area had been divided into five blocks. Block A, largely agricultural and containing eleven villages, including Naraina, Palam and Mahram Nagar, was reserved for the cantonment. Blocks C, D and E were earmarked for the future expansion of the city.

Block B, measuring over 13,000 acres, was the core of the new capital, the 'Imperial City area' where the government buildings would come up. This contained some areas of high population density, such as the hamlet of Jaisinghpura and nearby Madhoganj, within which some land was owned by the Maharaja of Jaipur. His ancestors had received these grants in Mughal times. Apart from these semi-urban areas, some 55 per cent of the land was cultivated. Most of the rest was locally known as *khandrat*, (literally, 'ruins'), because through it were scattered ruins, the remnants of various historical eras of the city. Also in this tract were some pockets of other economic activity, such as brick kilns, and even a derelict cotton mill in Raisina.

The acquisition proceedings created a class of the dispossessed, who were compensated in cash. Many non-agricultural people who had been expropriated due to the acquisition of the land on which their houses, shops or places of work or worship stood, usually found alternate pieces of land to relocate to. Some of these were allotted plots in new enclaves that were being developed for the purpose. For instance, a site of about twenty acres was allotted on the southeastern portion of land acquired for the new capital, for building of houses for 'expropriated menials and daily labourers'. The resulting settlement was developed along a strict grid layout, prescribed by the Imperial Delhi Committee and named after Mr Young, Deputy Commissioner. Soon, however, the name was corrupted, no doubt by residents who found more meaning in 'Jang'-pura than in 'Young'-pura.

It was not so easy for those who lost agricultural land. There was little land available for purchase within a reasonable distance of Delhi, particularly at the low rates they were given as compensation. In far-off areas such as the Canal Colonies in Punjab, land was available, but prices were even higher. Some agreed to accept this option, on the condition of paying for the land in instalments. While landowners and occupancy tenants were compensated, however inadequately, agricultural labourers were left without their source of livelihood, and without any compensation at all. Some of these, as well as owners whose lands had been acquired, continued to cultivate the land even after it had been acquired, as the government decided to let it out to them on short leases, until the land was actually needed for development. They thus became tenants of the government. To some extent, therefore, the government offset the cost of acquisition and prevented the loss of land revenue.

In the making of the new capital, much preliminary work had to be done even before the ground was broken. The appointment of the architects remained uncertain for a long time, a matter of careful negotiation. The creation of the administrative unit of Delhi prefigured the later Union Territory and the Delhi State as we know it today. Finally, the land for the building of the new capital was made available through a policy of extensive acquisitions. This is the land on which not only the imperial capital of New Delhi was built, but the future development of Delhi's 'colonies' would take place.

View from Humayun's Tomb; a photograph by Samuel Bourne, 1860s

New City on an Old Land

IN 1933, TWO YEARS AFTER THE INAUGURATION OF NEW DELHI, Baker would look back at a moment, more than twenty years before: 'I sat on the rock of Raisina which Lord Hardinge had chosen as the centre of New Delhi. The surroundings were very untidy, nothing but the little mud houses of the hamlet, the dust heaps, and the untidy foundations of many destroyed capitals; it all certainly seemed to justify what I think Lord Curzon said of it, "a deserted city of dreary and disconsolate tombs"…As we were looking down the great vista where it was planned to be…wondering how a great city could rise from such dreary surroundings, a perfect rainbow arch formed down the centre of that vista, appearing exactly where the great arch now is. We at once lost all doubt and acclaimed it as a great omen for the success of the new city.'

The site Baker and his companions looked out on, was indeed strewn with ruins. A major worry when a suitable site was being debated, was that this was 'man-worn' ground that might be difficult to build on. Many of these ruins were historic remnants of older cities of Delhi—ruined mosques, tombs and palaces. The site also contained a significant number of recently inhabited structures—the residences of those who had cultivated the land, and whose lands and houses had recently been acquired. To some extent the two categories overlapped. So, the villagers of Khairpur lived in the fifteenth- and sixteenth-century tombs and mosques that would later come to be Lodi Garden. Arab ki Sarai, adjacent to Humayun's Tomb, and Purana Qila, too, were inhabited.

Once the site was definitely settled on, one of the first tasks was to take stock of the structures that stood on it, with a view to assessing future action. The majority of the huts and houses of those who had been evacuated, were to be demolished. As for the historic structures, a list of 'mosques, temples and tombs' was prepared, in which these structures were grouped according to recommendations as to their eventual fate.

Forty-five structures were listed under the remark: 'Should be preserved'. These included several architecturally important structures such as Safdarjung's Tomb, Humayun's Tomb and Jantar Mantar. The list also included some architecturally less significant places, probably because they were in active use— such as graveyards, various Jain and

Hindu temples, mosques, dargahs and gurudwaras. The justification listed against most was couched in terms of it being a 'well-known place' or a 'famous place'.

Thirty-three buildings were recommended to 'not be destroyed unless destruction is imperative'. These included a number of buildings that were architecturally important or historically and/or culturally significant—the mosque known as Khair-ul-Manazil, Lal Bangla tombs, Feroz Shah Tughlaq's tomb in Hauz Khas, Gurudwara Bangla Sahib, the Hanuman temple on what is today Baba Kharak Singh Marg. Many of these were in use as places of worship and reverence, looked after by those who lived in the vicinity. It was thought that as these people were evicted from the localities, the sites would also lose their importance. An explanatory note thus added, 'probably in course of time they can be demolished as the expropriated people lose touch with the locality'.

Finally, the majority of buildings, a hundred and sixty-eight, it was felt, 'need not be preserved'. They included several temples and mosques, against some of which it was noted that the owners were willing to take compensation in return for the structure. Against one building, Najaf Khan's tomb, it was remarked that it was a large building in poor repair, and moreover 'the family is said to be—disloyal to Government during old times', as if to suggest that that was an added factor in allowing its demolition. It also listed buildings such as Agrasen's Baoli, and an unoccupied Bhairon Mandir near the Purana Qila. It was admitted that many more buildings and graves were actually in existence that had not been specifically mentioned, and would all fall into this category.

This preliminary list formed the foundation of a more detailed investigation, carried out by the Archaeological Survey of India (ASI) over the next few years. The result was a four-volume work, titled *List of Hindu and Mohammedan Monuments of Delhi Province*, today popularly known as the Zafar Hasan listing, after its author, who was an assistant superintendent in the ASI. The ASI list was more exhaustive than the 1912 list, both in terms of the historical and other detail, and in the number of buildings covered.

Though the 1912 list as well as the ASI's later list had dealt with all the land required for the new capital, immediate attention was only required for the cantonment and the core 'Imperial City area' where the main government buildings and residences were to be built. There were few historic structures within the cantonment area, and these were mostly located within villages such as Jharera, Nangal Raya, Mahram Nagar, which escaped destruction, even though the agricultural lands surrounding them were acquired for the use of the cantonment. The Imperial City area, on the other hand, was occupied by several villages and bastis (suburban settlements)—Khairpur, Babarpur, Bazidpur, Raisina, Narhaula, Sarban Sarai, Zabitaganj, Madhoganj, Jaisinghpura and Indarpat. The list of 1912 enumerated fifty-six historic structures here, and the ASI list, published in 1918, showed a total of eighty-three. However, out of those eighty-three, it listed only thirty-one as worthy of protection.

The ASI's recommendations were adopted selectively. For instance, a mosque at Zabitaganj, was deemed to be not worthy of protection by the ASI, but some Muslim members of the Legislative Council came forward in 1920 to protest against its demolition. As a result, it was left intact, to stand beside King's Way (now called Rajpath). On the other hand, certain 'ruins of palaces', believed to date from the time of Sher Shah Suri, abounding in 'subterranean vaults and passages', and recommended for protection, were cleared away. The main consideration here clearly was the greater importance given to religious sentiments of people using the place of worship, relative to the somewhat more academic historical importance of the archaeological site. Also, of course, the impracticality of preserving ruins which were evidently spread over a large area, in contrast to a more or less compact mosque, may also have been a consideration. The removal of certain structures that had been in use, but not considered of great historic importance, led to the relocation of their functions elsewhere. So, some places of worship were relocated, just as homes were. For instance, several temples in Jaisinghpura were relocated to premises in Paharganj.

Of those historic buildings that were preserved, important groups were incorporated into two large green areas—Lodi Garden and the Golf Course. A few important monuments would be given focal importance in the city's plan. Purana Qila, Safdarjung's Tomb, and Humayun's Tomb, were included as terminal points of important avenues, and thus became visual anchors for the layout. To fit into their new setting however, they needed a makeover. Purana Qila, for instance, housed the village of Indarpat, but this was demolished mid-1913, with the cooperation of the ASI which gave its opinion on which buildings were of archaeological importance, and

Arab ki Sarai, next to Humayun's tomb

would, therefore, be spared. In fact, considerable attention was given to the interior of Purana Qila—the open spaces were grassed, paths and roads were laid, a stepwell discovered in the grounds was conserved. Several other buildings of historic or religious importance were ultimately incorporated into green strips adjoining roads and plots.

The details of how major monuments would be incorporated into the town plan were worked out in consultation with Lutyens and Baker, who had been appointed general advisers to the committee on architectural matters concerning the new city. They were asked to give their opinions as to the design of approaches to Humayun and Safdarjung's tombs, the park around the Lodi tombs, the park around Jantar Mantar, Talkatora garden, the interior layout of Purana Qila, as well as the lake in front of it.

Eventually, the majority of structures, old and new, which were on the site earmarked for the Imperial City, were cleared away. By May 1913, most of the villages on the open ground destined to be the Imperial City had been evacuated, and demolitions had begun in the area that was to be the central vista. The clearing of the site produced an enormous quantity of stone. By mid-1913, some 60,000 cubic feet of stone had been collected from walls and ruins alone, before houses began to be demolished. This stone was used in the building of the new capital—in concrete and for making roads.

This was, to some extent, planned for. While project estimates were still being prepared, one of the preliminary tasks set out was 'clearings and levelling of interior of Indrapat, with a view to utilizing materials for roads'. The recycling of stones of older cities in the making of each new city had been a long tradition in the history of the city. Thus Sher Shah Suri had used the stones of Siri to build his city of Shergarh, and the city wall of Shahjahanabad had been partly built from the stones of Ferozabad, the city built by Feroz Shah Tughlaq in the mid-fourteenth century.

This use of recycled stone had an unexpected result on the plan of New Delhi. In the early plan, an amphitheatre carved out of the hillside had been placed west of Government House. It was felt that this would serve two purposes. The excavation would provide the large quantity of the hard Delhi quartzite stone that would be required for the building of New Delhi, and the depression left behind would be made into the amphitheatre, which could be used for future durbars. Since most of the requirement for stone for building material was met out of demolished structures, there was no need for excavation, and therefore, no resulting depression in the ground, hence the plan for an amphitheatre was dropped altogether!

While the task of clearing the land was taken in hand by the administration, the architects went ahead with their plans for the public buildings—Lutyens for Government House, and Baker for the Secretariat blocks. In March 1913, just as the final report of the Town Planning Committee was to be submitted, Lutyens, Baker and Hardinge came jointly to an important decision. This was that the Secretariat buildings as well as Government House would jointly occupy the elevated location of Raisina Hill, as opposed to the earlier idea that this spot would be reserved for Government House alone. The idea had originally come from Baker, who had couched it in

Houses awaiting demolition inside Purana Qila

terms of political symbolism—the powerful impact of having both the executive and administrative power of government elevated together to form 'one composition expressing unity in the instrument of Government.' Lutyens, and then Hardinge, agreed to this.

Though expressed in terms of universal principles, Baker's motivation was, no doubt, based largely on considerations of personal style. Swinton had once remarked: 'Whereas Lutyens seems to have a somewhat panicly (sic) fear of dealing with rock faces, Baker is accustomed to revel in them. Most of his buildings are on such rocky ground, and he likes to get rock effects and to make his buildings rise off and apparently grow out of rocky foundations.' The prospect of building his Secretariat blocks on a hill would be something Baker would have preferred. Baker was, in fact, quite excited about his 'platform', the cliff-like eastern edge of the two Secretariat buildings, and the wide flat court that stretched between them. In a letter to Hardinge, he claimed that he drew inspiration from the imperial architectural style of ancient Iran, and quoted from a book on the art of Persia, which described the Persepolis, built by Darius, thus: 'The object Darius had in view, when he set about erecting his stupendous platform was...to separate the King from the crowd and place his dwelling above their heads...with space and view at his command.'

So it was, that the two began to draw up their detailed plans. The issue of style, which had up to then been talked of in abstract terms and general principles, would now face the test of actual practice. Hardinge's primary concern, as he put it, was the inclusion of 'Indian thought and sentiment into the designs of our buildings, which I venture to regard as a consideration of very great political importance.' As to how this could best be done, he reminded them that this was the task for which Swinton Jacob, the advisor on 'Indian style', had expressly been appointed.

Even for Baker, who had expressed himself so eloquently on an ideal style for India, the starting point remained European classical architecture, adapted to the local climate and materials. On the foundations of European architecture, he felt, 'we must try to graft on…all that we can accept of what is best in Indian sentiment and achievement in art, and which does not conflict with our ideals.' Baker was diplomatic, in contrast to Lutyens, who did little to disguise his poor opinion of Indian architecture. He also thought little of the architectural talent of Swinton Jacob. Jacob, Lutyens complained, was pressing upon him structures 'covered with chuggas (chhajjas) and chattris', which Lutyens felt were 'anachronisms' to be avoided. The chhajja, a projecting stone cornice that was placed below a parapet to provide shade from the hot sun, and chhatris—cupolas supported on pillars, often placed on flat roofs—were characteristic features of Indian architecture, used generously in the Indo-Saracenic style, of which Jacob was a proponent. The conflicts between Jacob and Lutyens grew, until Jacob resigned, via a polite letter, in August 1913. Hardinge was sorry to see him go, suspecting that the resignation had much to do with Jacob being 'disgusted with the unreasonable attitude of Lutyens.'

Before leaving, Jacob put in a last word for the cause of

Indian architecture. In a note submitted to the India Office, he suggested that the way to incorporate the spirit of India in the architecture of New Delhi was through the involvement of Indian master builders in the imperial project. But this was not to be. Enthusiasm for an Indian style was generally lacking among officials who were involved with the project. Hailey, Chief Commissioner of Delhi, and the president of the Imperial Delhi Committee, expressed what must have been in many minds, when he said to Hardinge, 'Swinton Jacob's appointment had a value at the time it was made, in that it proved to the world that we were determined not to neglect the claims of Indian tradition.' Apparently, having once made the gesture and allayed public opinion, there was no need to follow through with substantial practical measures. It was finally decided that though there was a need to incorporate an Indian flavour into the architectural style of the new capital, one did not really need expert advice from Indians, or even those, like Jacob, who had some knowledge of Indian architecture. It was felt that Hardinge's advice and control over the two architects was quite enough to ensure that the required Indian motif would be adopted.

In general, the Government of India was unenthusiastic about the idea of having Indian master craftsmen take a lead in any part of the project. The argument was that Indian master builders did not work to any detailed drawings, and without any clear estimates as to time and cost. Under the circumstances, it would be best to put the skill of the Indian craftsmen under the direction of Western architecture, and of architects and engineers.

A press release from the government in 1914, took some pains to explain how the problem of style had been solved. It explained that 'the task set to the architects was not to produce a group of buildings of any particular style, but to design a capital which should be structurally adopted for the uses for which it is required, and at the same time in keeping with the great monuments of India's past with which it is surrounded'. It had been decided that the Indian element would be kept at the superficial level of adornment alone. This was explained away by the assertion that 'the peculiar genius of the Indian workman lies in ornament and decoration'. It was a happy coincidence that Indian craftsmen could be employed more cheaply than Europeans, for instance, in stone carving.

The relationship between Western architecture and Indian decorative arts, which came to characterize the buildings of the new capital, according to one scholar, represents the essence and problem of Hardinge's political programme for India's future. The Indian spirit would run through the city, but not be the dominant inspiration, just as, 'though deserving greater involvement in the colonial government, India always would be a junior imperial partner'. In its Final Report, submitted in 1913, the Town Planning Committee had captured the spirit behind the plan of New Delhi—it had 'to convey the idea of connection with the Delhi of the past and a peaceful domination and dignified rule over the traditions and life of India by the British Raj'.

The Central Vista, 1951

The Garden City

THE DEBATE OVER THE SITE AND STYLE OF MAJOR administrative and ceremonial buildings tended to attract the most official and public attention, but of no less significance were the other components of the city's plan. The planning of a city on what was more or less a tabula rasa, was both an opportunity and a responsibility. The exercise reflected the planners' vision for the new imperial capital, and an understanding of the physical, social, economic and cultural needs of those who would inhabit it.

Of the various possible models available to colonial planners, one might have been the Mughal city of Shahjahanabad. This, too, was a planned city, founded in the seventeenth century by Shahjahan as an imperial capital. The influence this had on New Delhi was, however, limited to the question of how best to connect (or not) the Mughal and British cities, or the idea of incorporating views such as that of the Jama Masjid into the vistas of the new city. Not surprisingly, the planners instead looked to the examples of 'modern' towns; towns that were suitable for a European as opposed to a 'native' population, whose needs were deemed to be quite different.

In Britain itself there were, as yet, no examples of comprehensive modern town planning by the government. There was, on the other hand, a new idea that was catching on in the sphere of private sector development—that of the 'garden city'. The garden city movement was based on the ideas of Ebenezer Howard, developed in a book called *Garden Cities of Tomorrow*, which was published in 1902. Howard's ideas were a reaction against the rapid urbanization of his time, which had led to haphazard development, overcrowding and squalor. The garden city, as an antidote to this poor quality of urban life, sought to combine the positive aspects of rural and urban living, by designing a city where people would be close to nature, while at the same time enjoying all the economic, civic, cultural and social amenities of a city. The idea of people living close to nature, in small manageable urban communities, was at the core of the concept.

The idea of the garden city, though new, had rapidly become a watchword in town planning. George Swinton himself had been involved in the planning of the very first garden city in England, Letchworth, on which construction had begun in 1903. Lutyens had made important contributions to the design of the central square in Hampstead Garden Suburb, another privately developed garden city, built shortly after. For Delhi, the idea of a garden city had begun to be talked about even before the constitution of the Town Planning Committee. Louis Dane, the Lieutenant Governor of Punjab, in a note dated 11 January 1912, had said that he 'presumed the new Government Capital should be...a large and spacious garden city.' He also suggested that 'some of the old monuments, e.g. Safdarjung and the Lodhi tombs, could be enclosed in a fine park which would form a good central feature.'

But the garden city, as it was interpreted in the town plan of New Delhi, was very different from the original concept. One obvious difference was in the monumental complex of government buildings, and in the majestic ceremonial avenue. These were inspired by older capital cities, such as Washington and Paris, which had shown the way by grouping important state buildings and monuments along grand ceremonial avenues. Other features were taken from India's own history. From the advent of the East India Company, most colonial towns had been divided into the 'Civil Lines'—inhabited largely by the European population; the 'native town'—usually an older settlement, inhabited by the indigenous population; and the cantonment. The new capital did not depart from this pattern. New Delhi proper was comparable in function to the older Civil Lines. It was flanked on the southwest by a large new cantonment. On the northeast lay the older Mughal city of Shahjahanabad, now relegated to being 'Old Delhi', and housing the bulk of the Indian population.

The segregation between the predominantly British elite and indigenous population was a sharp departure from the community living ideal of the garden city, as developed by Ebenezer Howard and others, and applied to neighbourhoods such as Letchworth and Hampstead Garden Suburb. Segregation was a deeply ingrained premise of colonial rule, which the British Raj failed to break free from, despite the apparent espousal of political reform as a policy. Lutyens wrote: 'The natives do not improve much on acquaintance. Their very low intellects spoil much and I do not think it possible for the Indians and whites to mix freely and naturally. They are very different and even my ultra-wide sympathy with them cannot admit them on the same plane as myself.'

Yet, the realities of the colonial state and society were more complex than a simple division between the Civil Lines and the native town would suggest. The estimates of the numbers that the city was expected to accommodate, tell the story quite well. While it was expected that some 5,000 Europeans, both official and non-official, would live in the city, the number of Indians was expected to be 40,000. The lower echelons of the British Indian administrative machinery had long employed a number of Indians, for instance, in clerical positions. More lately, numbers of Indians within the colonial upper bureaucracy, the civil service, were also growing, and this process speeded up particularly from the 1920s. Besides, many of the menial and other services were provided by Indians.

It soon became clear that these various categories of Indians, closely associated with the government machinery and its personnel, had to be accommodated within New Delhi. An exchange of correspondence regarding the subordinate staff of the Viceregal Estate reveals the issues involved. It was anticipated that Indians would by and large prefer to live in Old Delhi, despite the distance from the new city. This, however, was considered undesirable on two grounds. One, on 'medical and sanitary grounds', to prevent the 'introduction of infectious and contagious diseases on to the Estate'. It was assumed that the old 'native town' was a sinkhole of infection and unsanitary conditions, and the daily contact between it and New Delhi, via Indian staff travelling to and fro, was dangerous to the health of the European population of the new city. The second reason was 'the greater control that could be exercised over the various establishments...if they were resident on the Estate'. It was therefore decided that rent-free accommodation had to be provided on the estate, to induce the subordinate staff to live there.

Similar arguments, no doubt, lay behind the government's decision to provide accommodation for the majority of its employees, both European and Indian, within New Delhi. As a result, government-built residential space constituted a large proportion of the area in the town plan, and on this the town planners had to work closely with officialdom. This was because British society in India, particularly in an administrative centre such as Delhi, was largely stratified on the basis of government rank and pay scale. In the hierarchy of civil servants, each official's rank determined the size of their residential space. Government housing in the new capital followed a plan that took into account the hierarchies of colonial bureaucracy. Residences for officers were categorized into six 'classes', distinguished not only by size but by quality of construction. Residences for clerks were an even more complex issue, with four classes for European clerks, and five classes for Indian clerks.

The bungalows in general were set in large compounds ranging in size from one to three acres. The main reason for the large size of plots was the need to accommodate within each compound a large staff of Indian servants, estimated at twenty-two per bungalow. Not only did enough housing need to be provided for them; their quarters also had to be kept at a safe distance from the main house; a distance necessary 'on account of noise and on sanitary grounds'. Indians, particularly of a lower social and economic class, while they were accommodated in the new city, could still be physically segregated. Government House was set in the largest compound of all, occupying over 300 acres. It included various levels of accommodation for a number of staff, as well as the lines of the Viceroy's Bodyguard. The provision of generous compounds contributed to a low density of population in New Delhi, i.e. 10.8 per acre, compared to the 21.25 per acre for the average city in the United Provinces, and even compared to the density of population in London, which ranged from 14.8 to 22.7 per acre.

Decreasing rank in the administrative hierarchy meant an increasing distance from the central forum or administrative hub. So, for example, the highest officials—Members of the Viceroy's Council, were accommodated in large bungalows closest to the Secretariat. The clerks' quarters were at the outer edges, north of the Central Vista. In this category, the racial principles on which colonial bureaucracy was organized, became most apparent. Among the clerks, Indians and Anglo-Indians (i.e. Europeans) were both equally well represented, but were treated very unequally. For instance, an Anglo-Indian clerk would live in a house twice the size of an Indian in the same pay grade.

The discriminatory nature of this arrangement was not lost on those for whom this accommodation was meant. Chandra Narayan Mathur, a clerk in the Home Department, wrote a letter to Hardinge on the subject. He pointed out the several deficiencies in the housing proposed for Indian clerks, such as the lack of a dining room, and the fact that the bathrooms and toilets were poorly built and not attached to the main house. He deplored this 'unequal treatment', which he said, was 'felt as a mark of inferiority by Indians as a class.' This representation, though embarrassing, did not change the planners' decision.

One category that occupied a special racial and class position was that of the 'native princes', the rulers of semi-independent monarchical states of India. This indigenous elite class was an important part of the colonial state and society. Soon after the planning of the new city began, the princes began to make applications to be allotted land in the new capital. This, felt Hardinge, was to be encouraged in order to foster their ties with the imperial government. With

Jaipur House

the growth of the national movement, the princes were seen as a bulwark of the British Raj. The princes were, therefore, given (or actually allowed to purchase) generous plots, ranging in area from four to eight acres. In the early estimates it was calculated that some seventy-five 'Indian chiefs villa residences' would occupy a total of some 500 acres of land.

The princes' placement was in a prominent position, around Princes' Park—an area that would later come to be known popularly as India Gate. At the same time, they were segregated, at the far end of the Central Vista, at a considerable distance from Raisina Hill. An important consideration here was, as Hardinge put it, to keep the rulers' 'numerous and motley followers' at a distance from the centre of power.

New Delhi thus came to accommodate a number of

Indians, from the Indian rulers and their employees, to those in government employment, and those who lived in servants' quarters in the spacious bungalow compounds. Apart from these, however, there was a large number of Indians who worked in unorganized menial jobs to serve the domestic and civic needs of New Delhi. They ultimately came to live mostly in Paharganj. This settlement, the demolition of which had once been contemplated, thus came to serve a very important function within a society highly stratified and segregated along lines of class and race.

Size and quality of accommodation, and location, were not the only indicators of hierarchy within colonial society. Nomenclature played an equally important role. When it came to naming roads, at the top of the scale lay the British monarch and the royal family. The most important road in the city, connecting Government House to Princes' Park, also described as the 'Central Vista', was 'King's Way' (Rajpath). Bisecting this road at right angles was 'Queen's Way' (now called Janpath). Important roads, that is, those on which the houses of the higher echelons of the government were located, were named after British monarchs: 'Prince Edward Place' (Vijay Chowk), 'King Edward Road' (Maulana Azad Road), 'Queen Victoria Road' (Dr Rajendra Prasad Road), 'Queen Mary's Avenue' (Pandit Pant Marg), 'King George's Avenue' (Rajaji Marg). Two large junctions of roads were named 'York Place' (Motilal Nehru Place), and 'Windsor Place', and of course, the main shopping centre was named 'Connaught Place', after the Duke of Connaught, the uncle of George V.

The second rung of streets was named after important figures in the history of the establishment of Britain's power in India: 'Clive Road' (Tyagaraj Marg), and 'Hastings Road' (Krishna Menon Road). Interestingly, icons of other European colonial powers in India were also acknowledged with important roads: the French general, Dupleix (K. Kamraj Marg), and the Portuguese Afonso de Albuquerque (Tees January Marg). There were also predictably a large number of roads named after Governors General and Viceroys (and some wives)—past, present, and those that would come in the future and have roads named after them: Hardinge (Tilak Marg), Cornwallis (Subramanya Bharti Marg), Wellesley (Zakir Hussain Marg), Dalhousie (Dara Shikoh Road), Canning (Madhav Rao Scindia Marg), Lytton (Copernicus Marg), Curzon (Kasturba Gandhi Marg), Lady Hardinge (Shaheed Bhagat Singh Marg), Chelmsford, Reading (Mandir Marg), Irwin (Baba Kharak Singh Marg), Willingdon (Mother Teresa Crescent) and Linlithgow (Professor Ram Nath Vij Marg).

On the third rung, minor thoroughfares or those in neighbourhoods housing clerks or others of a lower strata, were named after military figures, such as Henry Havelock and John Nicholson, or those who were closely associated with the construction or early administration of New Delhi. Hence there was 'Hailey Road', and 'Lutyens Road'.

Just as the Indian princes had been given a special position as regards location and size of plot, Indian rulers and ruling dynasties too were acknowledged in the toponymy of the new capital. This was not surprising, since the aim was to connect this new Empire of India to the line of previous empires in this ancient land, particularly those that had been centred at Delhi. This principle governed the naming of several of the roads leading off Princes' Park (where the houses of the Indian states' rulers were located), and some beyond: Feroz Shah, Ashoka, Humayun, Akbar, Shahjahan, Aurangzeb, Sher Shah, Lodi, Prithvi Raj, Tughlaq. The Marathas, who had controlled Delhi in the late eighteenth century, were acknowledged through roads: Scindia Road and Peshwa Road, both in the clerks' quarters north of Government House.

The Rajput ruler Man Singh was also honoured with a road, probably because of the Jaipur state's long association with Delhi. Man Singh had been granted land by the Mughals in the capital, where he had built a Hanuman temple, and near which his descendant Jai Singh had built the observatory known as Jantar Mantar. These hereditary lands, which formed the settlements of Jaisinghpura and Madho Ganj, had been acquired for building the capital. A road close to Jantar Mantar was named after Jai Singh.

Old landmarks lent their names to a few roads. One was Kushak Road, named after the Kushak-e-Shikar, a hunting lodge and adjoining embankment constructed by the emperor Feroz Shah Tughlaq in the fourteenth century. Old Mill Road (now Rafi Ahmed Kidwai Marg) was named after a derelict cotton mill that had stood near Raisina. Raisina itself gave its name to a road.

One road that came to be named by accident was Pandara Road. It appears on the earliest official maps of the capital that show road names, for instance, the Delhi Guide Map of 1933, and has continued thus till today. It has surprisingly been accepted all these years without question. This was a question that troubled A.V. Askwith, Chief Commissioner, Delhi, in 1942. On enquiry, the response that he received from the president of the New Delhi Municipal Corporation (NDMC) was, that it was probably supposed to be 'Pandava', after the mythical heroes of ancient India. The naming of one of New Delhi's roads after the Pandavas was not unexpected, as Purana Qila, where the Central Vista terminated, was believed to be the very site of Indraprastha, the capital city founded by the Pandavas in the ancient past. However, when the list of roads was made up, the handwritten lower case 'v' in 'Pandava' had been erroneously typed up by some clerk as 'r', and the mistake was never corrected!

The town plan, in terms of how the roads were laid out, was quite distinctive. A scheme of hexagons and equilateral triangles was adopted, and the roads consequently radiated from multiple roundabouts. In a speech in 1933, Lutyens acknowledged Hardinge's role in determining this as well as other details of the city's plan, saying, 'The new city owes its being to Lord Hardinge...His command that one Avenue should lead to Purana Kila (Indrapat) and another to the Jumma Masjid was the father of the equilateral and hexagonal plan. This was a sorry nuisance to all whose thoughts could not merge beyond the right angles of New York...'

Hardinge was also concerned about the width of the roads. He felt that the initial proposals from the architects had allowed for roads that were too wide. He, therefore, looked for models elsewhere. On 19 July 1913, he wrote to the Maharaja of Jaipur, Madho Singh, asking to be informed of the breadth of the principal streets of the city, expecting from this knowledge, 'great assistance' in deciding upon the width of the streets to be made in the new city of Delhi. In response, the Maharaja sent a plan of the city, adding that it was 'indeed a great honour to the old city of Jaipur, designed and built at a time when the science of town-planning was in its infancy.' These plans Hardinge studied, noting that the streets of Jaipur varied from 123 to 107 feet in width. He suggested to Hailey that the streets of Delhi, excepting the main avenue, not be made much wider than this.

One feature that did give New Delhi at least the look, very literally, of a 'garden city', was its large number of trees. The large compounds of the bungalows were each planted with several large trees. Trees were also planted along each avenue. The choosing of trees for the avenues was a matter for careful consideration, and decisions were taken by Lutyens and the Director of Horticulture, W.R. Mustoe. The size and shape of each of the species had to be in proportion to the width of the road they would stand beside. Further, 'Because orientation in a hexagonal road system was more difficult for every road user than in a normal rectangular system, it seemed right to give every road an unmistakable "botanic footprint".' Thus Aurangzeb Road was planted exclusively with neem, and Akbar Road with tamarind.

It was not just in gardens and beside roads that trees were being planted. The Ridge, which lay along the western edge of the city, would have to be transformed. As it was, it

Lodi Garden today

presented a rather barren prospect, described as being largely rocky, with small patches of soil between the stones, 'which support shrubs and bushes and throw up grass in the rainy season'. This vegetation was heavily grazed by goats and sheep. The idea of afforestation of the Ridge, and turning it into a reserved forest, was first examined in mid-1912, when the idea of placing Government House on the Ridge had been briefly considered. The later report of the Town Planning Committee, while it placed Government House east of the Ridge itself, saw the Ridge as forming an important part of the city, in the shape of a green spine. A scheme was now devised for the afforestation of this barren tail end of the Aravalli range of ancient mountains. Rough terraces would be made to hold up soil, and natural watercourses would be modified to provide efficient irrigation. Scenic drives would be constructed on the higher parts, and it was envisaged that, 'The panorama of the present city, the new city and the monuments and cities of the past stretching below to the river as seen from the rough eminence past a foreground of rocks and trees should be one difficult to match for charm.'

As the discussion about the possibility of afforestation on the Ridge progressed, conservators of forests consulted local residents familiar with the Ridge, to understand this natural feature, its soil, climate and flora and fauna. Two of these local experts were named in their report: Malfak and Jhabbar Khan, Mewatis of Rikabganj. These men had been positive about the quality of the soil, even suggesting that irrigation would not be required as long as grazing was prevented. After this consultation, a list of seventy-two trees suitable for planting had been prepared. One of the entries on the list of 1912, was a species listed under the botanical name *Pithecellobium dulce*. This was a tree popularly known as jangal jalebi, but on the list its popular name, no doubt erroneously, was written as wilayati kikar. The tree actually known as wilayati kikar, known to botanists as *Prosopis juliflora*, did not figure on the list. It is ironic that this tree, probably not originally recommended for plantation on the Ridge, was later to be extensively used and would become a weed in this extensive area.

Visitors to New Delhi today often remark on how green the centre of the city is. This 'garden city' owed its origins to a variety of factors—a new town planning concept that had its beginnings in early twentieth-century Britain, colonial ideas of sanitation and segregation, and the presence of a natural feature, the Ridge.

Human, animal and machine power at work

Building in Fits and Starts

IN APRIL 1914, IN AN ARTICLE WRITTEN FOR PUBLICATION IN the *Times of India*, Hailey acknowledged that more than two years had gone by since the transfer of the capital had been announced, and 'as the months went on, there must have been those who found something peculiarly apposite in the old Persian proverb—*Dilhi dur ast*, "Delhi is still a long way off".'

The time had been spent in the process of fixing a site, acquiring and clearing the land, and appointing the architects. By late 1913, some work had been achieved on the ground as well. The material collected from demolished buildings was being used to construct roads, the ground was being levelled, machinery was being put together, nursery gardens were being set up, and light railways were being laid for convenient transportation of material. Further progress was dependent on a complex coordination between the architects, the Imperial Delhi Committee, the engineers of the Public Works Department, the Government of India, and the Secretary of State for India in London. This coordination was complicated by the fact that Lutyens and Baker spent only two or three months each year in Delhi, during the winter.

One concern that arose right from the beginning was the projected cost of the government buildings. Hardinge declared himself 'rather horrified at the prodigious estimates' that were being prepared. At the same time, it was felt that the buildings of New Delhi had to be worthy of an Imperial City. Harcourt Butler, a Member of the Viceroy's Council, argued, 'we have to make New Delhi one of the world's wonders and topics of conversation!' After some pruning, an estimate that projected a total cost of Rs. 9,17,04,300, or 6,113,620 pounds sterling for the construction works in the new city, was arrived at by March 1914, and these were soon approved by the Secretary of State for India in London.

In the meanwhile, the architects had been given lists of the requirements of space for each of the various government departments that had to be accommodated, and they got busy with the task of designing. While their plans were awaited, the Public Works Department was eager to push ahead with the construction. One task that could be completed even in the absence of final plans, was the preparation of the top of Raisina Hill to accommodate the Secretariat buildings and

Government House. This was accomplished in early 1914, and it was decided that the task of building up retaining walls and foundations could begin. To enable this to be done, some basic parameters had to be decided. On the one hand, the slope of the road as it rose up to the Secretariat and Government House was to be determined. At a meeting attended by both Lutyens and Baker, the committee decided that the gradient would be fixed at a maximum of '1 in 25' (a maximum increase of one foot in height for every twenty-five feet in distance). Also, to enable work on the foundations to begin, it was necessary to know the final position and exterior dimensions of the buildings. By March 1914, both Lutyens and Baker had agreed and signed off on these details as well. This was to have a crucial significance for later developments.

The pace of construction nevertheless continued to be adversely affected by several factors. One bottleneck was the slow supply of stone. Arrangements had been made for the supply of stone from quarries in Rajasthan—red sandstone from Bharatpur and Dholpur, and buff sandstone from Dholpur. The red sandstone required for the base of the Secretariat blocks was being supplied from Bharatpur at half the speed anticipated. Though special railway lines were laid to access the mines, through agreements with the states concerned, the supply of stone continued to be a problem in the years to come. The architects' insistence on a bright shade of red meant that a relatively small percentage of the stone quarried was actually acceptable. On the other hand, the supply of bricks was an easier matter. Brick kilns came up all over the site of the future

New Delhi. Located in their vicinity were coolie-lines—rows of quarters built to house those who worked in them.

An added problem was the outbreak of World War I, in the middle of 1914. Material that had to be imported from England, such as machinery, was delayed, as supply lines and freight charges were affected. Many of the engineers of the PWD left for Europe to contribute to the war effort. By 1915, the adverse financial effects of the war were also beginning to be felt, as the government's yearly budget allocation for the New Delhi project was reduced, from 60 lakhs to 40 lakhs, though Hardinge got an informal assurance that an additional sanction of up to 10 lakhs could be obtained. By early 1916, the effect of price rises because of the war was also throwing the budget estimates out of gear.

By the end of 1914, some progress had been made on the foundations of the Secretariat, though in Hardinge's opinion, not as much as he had hoped. While appreciative of the fact that a lot of spadework, very literally, had gone into the preparation of Raisina Hill, Hardinge was worried that there was not enough to show by way of structures. He worried that this gave critics of the project another thing to complain about. The problem was, that there were still many, such as Curzon, who were questioning the need to build a new city. Hardinge quite rightly felt that if actual structures began to be seen, the project would quite literally be set in stone, for it would be considered a loss of face to abandon the construction.

This reasoning was proved to be valid two years later, when Hardinge was replaced as Viceroy by Lord Chelmsford.

Special railway transporting material

Chelmsford, though not as personally committed to the idea of building the new capital, realized that, 'In as much as there had been seven cities of Delhi in the past which had been completed by the monarchs who had established them, it was impossible to conceive of an eighth city of Delhi commenced under his Majesty's auspices and abandoned. It would be a fatal blow to the prestige of the British Raj to leave ruins as colossal as any of the old cities and as an example for all time of the inability of British rule to create a new Capital.' Clearly then, as soon as structures actually began to be built, the future of the city was assured.

Factors such as the war were worrying setbacks to Hardinge's aim of building enough structures to make the project irreversible, but what could not be achieved in volume, could be compensated for in the weight of symbolism. It was decided that the foundation stones that had been laid at the Durbar site in December 1911, would be moved to Raisina and installed as commemoration stones in chambers built into the bases of the towers at the eastern ends of the Secretariat blocks. This was done in a small ceremony on 31 July 1915, attended by Hardinge. Now, surely, the promise of the new city was firmly and irreversibly anchored in the soil of Delhi.

Despite the disruptions caused by the war, work on building foundations and retaining walls for Government House and the Secretariat blocks progressed through 1915. Railings and water fountains had begun to appear in the forecourt in front of Government House, when, in early February 1916, an unexpected controversy arose. Lutyens raised a question about the gradient of the road that led up to Government House from the 'Great Place' or 'Great Court' (today known as Vijay Chowk). As designed, the road began an upward slope west of the Great Court, climbed up to the Secretariat buildings, and then continued flat to Government House. Lutyens pointed out that the design was such that the view of Government House was obstructed by the crest of the inclined road, as it came up to the Secretariat buildings. This, he claimed, was a violation of the original concept of the design, which was based on a view of Government House, framed between the Secretariat blocks, from the Great Court. The only solution was to alter the gradient, and extend the slope evenly, further west towards Government House.

Baker, in opposition to this, declared that this plan was unfeasible. It would involve cutting through the raised platform that had been designed as a bridge between the Secretariat buildings, modelled on the 'stupendous platform' of Darius at Persepolis, which he had praised to Hardinge in 1913. This platform, he further claimed, had been agreed upon between the architects and the committee long ago. The obscuring of the view of Government House from the Great Court was an inevitable result that should have been clear to Lutyens from the beginning.

The committee was inclined to support Baker's position regarding this, on two main grounds. One was for a very practical reason. A view of Government House from the Great Court could only be achieved by cutting through the crest of the hill, and in effect, through the platform that connected the two Secretariat blocks. This would disrupt the easy connectivity between them. Instead of flat ground, officials and others going from one building to another, would have to go down and then up twenty-four steps in the centre of the blocks, and thirty-five steps at the eastern end of the blocks. This would mean that the Secretariat blocks would cease to function as one unit. Moreover, the alteration would involve extra expense, to the tune of some one-and-a-half lakh rupees.

Secondly, the committee felt that Lutyens had no just cause to complain. They pointed out that he had himself filed a plan in early 1914 which showed the gradient terminating before the Secretariat blocks. Both he and Baker had also filed plans of the positions of the buildings on the layout plan. In addition, in the summer of 1913, W.H. Nicholls, the architect member of the committee, had produced a perspective sketch, which had made it very clear that from the Great Court only the dome of Government House would be seen. The one misleading piece of the whole picture was one of a set of watercolours that had been prepared by the artist William Walcot, for exhibition at the Royal Academy in London in 1914. This showed a panorama viewed from the Great Court, showing Government House appearing between the Secretariats. This was clearly inaccurate, but, the committee felt, they could not be held to the artist's vision, but would go by the specifications submitted by the architects.

Lutyens, while he agreed that he had signed off on the final plans, confessed that it was an error made in good faith. He had seriously believed that Government House would be fully visible from the Great Court. He lamented the fact that Nicholl's perspective view had not been shared with the architects. This communication gap was, in fact, an unintended result of the practice of the architects to depart for England every year as soon as the summer set in, while the committee continued its work in India. Lutyens probably only got a realistic idea of the result on the ground as the construction of the platform between the Secretariat buildings progressed.

In any event, Hardinge, too, agreed with the committee that the decision had been taken more than two years previously, and had been agreed to by all concerned, saying that he considered it 'little short of a scandal that, after the acceptance of the architects' plans two years ago, a divergence of opinion upon an obvious but material point in those same plans should now be raised.' He categorically rejected

Lutyens' proposal for cutting a slope between the Secretariat buildings to correct what he considered a defect.

The slope question was one of Hardinge's last important interventions on the New Delhi project. His five-year term, which ought to have come to an end in November 1915, had been extended by six months due to the uncertainties of the war, and the resulting desire to have some continuity and stability in India. He left Delhi on the last day of March 1916, to be succeeded by Chelmsford as Viceroy. Among the many farewell gifts Hardinge received, was a particularly appropriate one from the Imperial Delhi Committee—a volume of photographs of the work in progress at Delhi, with a promise of further photographs to be mailed to him, to apprise him of the progress being made. On his part, he promised, 'my interest in New Delhi will never wane; and...I am quite determined to return some day to Delhi to see the new city when completed.'

The Capitol complex was of course just one part, albeit an important part, of the new capital. Residential accommodation for government employees was another part of the project that was a matter for deliberation. Just as there had been a debate as to whether important public buildings, including Government House and the Secretariat, be built by competition or by the nomination of architects, the question of how bungalows and other government quarters would be designed, also needed to be worked out. To begin with, official opinion was in favour of competition, but when this failed to bring forth any workable designs, it was decided that Baker and Lutyens would submit plans

Bricks being made

for various types of bungalows, and they in fact submitted several designs for bungalows—large and small, flat-roofed and tiled. From mid-1914, to the end of 1915, several sample designs of gazetted officers' bungalows were constructed.

Eventually, both Lutyens' and Baker's designs were deemed too expensive to implement. The need for economy was a compelling reason why eventually the bulk of the government bungalows in New Delhi were finally designed, under the overall supervision of Lutyens and Baker, by the Public Works Department, and some by the architect member of the Imperial Delhi Committee. The latter position was first occupied by W.H. Nicholls, and then by R.T. Russell. Based on these plans, bungalows designed for Members of the Viceroy's Council, and the Commander-in-Chief's bungalow, were completed in 1925 and 1930 respectively.

Lutyens, however, did design bungalows as part of 'Schedule B' of Government House. Schedule B was located in the northwest corner of the Viceregal compound, and comprised a number of subsidiary buildings that would be needed for the numerous and varied staff of Government House. The accommodation, all of which was to be designed by Lutyens, included a bungalow for the Private Secretary to the Viceroy, and one for his Military Secretary; and a number of other public buildings, including stables and garages. Later a mirror image of Schedule B, now confusingly called Schedule A, was built to the southwest of Government House, to house the personnel of the President's Bodyguard.

Outside the Viceregal Estate, work on residences at the lower end of the scale, that of clerks' quarters, had commenced much earlier, in January 1914. This was deemed to be a less complicated task, and the government had been eager to start work on this without wasting too much time. One reason why this part of the project was given priority was that until the Secretariat buildings were functional and the clerks moved into their quarters in New Delhi, many of these quarters could in the meantime house engineering staff working on the construction of New Delhi. As the staff came to reside in this area, the need for the necessities of daily life was also felt. At first temporary stalls came up, and hawkers were given permission to sell. By 1921, the hexagonal market, which soon came to be known as Round (Gole) Market, was built to provide a permanent commercial centre for the area.

On the major government buildings, which had suffered most from the disruption caused by World War I, the pace of construction picked up slowly once the war came to an end. An added worry was that prices had risen considerably as a consequence of the war. The estimates for the entire project, which had been calculated at around 917 lakh rupees before the war, were finally put at 1,419 lakh rupees.

While some progress was made on the Secretariat buildings after the end of the war, Government House lagged behind. Though the stone supply from Dholpur had speeded up, it still could not keep up with the demand, particularly as the Bharatpur supply was still scanty. So, a choice had to be made, and priority was accorded to the Secretariats, to enable various government departments to start functioning from their permanent quarters as soon as possible. Therefore, the limited stone was diverted to the construction of the

Secretariats at the cost of Government House. As a result, work on the Secretariats progressed well, and in 1925, several departments started moving into the buildings. By November 1926, the Secretariat was fully functional within its new premises, even though the domes were yet to be built. The buildings were finally completed only in 1930.

Government House was not the only building to suffer. In 1924, the foundations of the Record Office and a War Memorial Arch (which is now popularly known as India Gate) had been laid, but the very next year the supply of stone to these structures too was stopped. Between the two, the Record Office was given priority, and was made ready for partial occupation in October 1926, even though some work remained to be completed. Work on the arch made slower progress. Some of the details of the carving, and the teak doors were finally finished in 1932, after the monument had already been inaugurated.

Priority, in terms of supply of stone, was also given to

Blasting Raisina Hill

a new 'Legislative building' on which work had begun in 1921. This building, which we know today as Parliament House, where the Lok Sabha and Rajya Sabha now meet, had not been a part of the original plan. The question of where the Chamber of Princes and the Imperial Legislative Council —the two bodies with a legislative role, would convene, had been raised in the early stages of the planning process. Hardinge had been adamant that both these legislative bodies would be housed under the roof of Government House. There was a political symbolism at stake here. These bodies were advisory at best, without any independence, and under the firm control of the Viceroy. Their location within Government House reaffirmed this relationship. When it came to allowing Indians a greater share in the empire, the government was only willing to go so far.

This idea had been questioned even in 1912. Arthur Murray, a member of the House of Commons, argued for a separate council building, as 'an outward and visible sign of the new era of political development in which the peoples of India must wisely be guided to take an increasingly larger share.' While at the time Murray's suggestion was not acceptable to the government, by 1919 the situation had changed. The Government of India Act, 1919, was a response to the growing demands of Indians for increased participation in the political process. The Viceroy had, up to this point, held both executive and legislative powers, though in the latter he was 'advised' by his council. Legislative powers were now to be vested in a Council of State, or upper house, and a Legislative Assembly, or lower house.

This separation of powers had to be reflected in a physical

separation between the building housing the Viceroy and that in which the legislature would sit. It became necessary, therefore, to design a new Council House. The location that was chosen was at the foot of Raisina Hill, though space could have been carved out of the vast compound of Government House. This physical placement of the legislature building has been seen by some scholars as an articulation of the premise of the British empire—Indian participation, though growing, had still to be subordinated to British power—focused in the Government House and the Secretariat on Raisina Hill. The Legislative building, designed by Baker, was formally opened on 18 January 1927, though there was still some finishing to be done on the Chamber of Princes.

Construction began at the same time on two large blocks of hostels to house the legislators who would be visiting Delhi for the lengths of time that the assemblies were in session. These came to be known as Western Court and Eastern Court, designed by Robert Tor Russell, and built across from each other on Queen's Way. Not far from these, off Windsor Place (on Feroz Shah Road) 'twenty sets of single orthodox quarters' were built for the accommodation of Indian members of the legislature. Within a year however it was decided that more 'orthodox quarters' would be needed, and to finance these, the Eastern Court was sold off to the Post and Telegraph Department.

When work on the Secretariat and Legislative buildings was nearing completion, attention was once again turned to Government House. The four wings of the house were completed in 1928 and the dome was put in the following year, though the deep chhajja posed some technical difficulties. Other unexpected hiccups included a frost in January 1929, which killed off many plants in the newly planted garden. Finally, on 23 December 1929, the Viceroy, Lord Irwin (who had succeeded Chelmsford in 1926), moved into the house, even though some electrical works remained to be completed. Early that year, it had been decided, by George V himself, that the official name of Government House would be changed to Viceroy's House.

As the construction on buildings had progressed, so had the task of planting the large number of trees that were a part of the city plan—along the avenues, in residential compounds and in public gardens. A plant nursery for the supply of trees was set up in Jorbagh. Maintenance of the planted saplings was a constant concern, not only due to the need to provide adequate irrigation, but because, as it was remarked in 1922, 'the maintenance of trees and gardens was still hampered by the depredations of stray cattle.' The making of roads had been an early task of the builders of the city, not simply as the streets of the final layout, but as arteries through which construction material, labour and supervisors could travel. Their final finishing was accomplished once the major government buildings were nearing completion and occupation. The electrification of the main streets was completed in 1925, and the rest in 1928.

When the project had commenced in 1912 with the appointment of the Town Planning Committee, no one could have anticipated that it would take nearly two decades before the city was ready for inauguration. In retrospect, however, even without the unexpected setbacks such as the war, there was the sheer magnitude of the project—the acquisition of land, planning of the details of the monumental public buildings, the preparation of the ground, the provision of money, material, machinery and manpower. New Delhi, much like Rome, could not be built in a day.

The Secretariat; a photograph from 15 August 1947

New Delhi Unveiled

IN THE MONTH OF FEBRUARY 1931, THE NEW CAPITAL WAS ready for a formal inauguration. It had reached completion despite the many setbacks and tribulations encountered during its planning and construction. The need for a transfer of the capital and indeed for constructing a city at all had been questioned from the start of the process right up to the end of World War I. There were frequent complaints about the expense involved, from British political and commercial circles, both in Britain and in India. An unexpected support for the project came from Indians themselves. A motion had been introduced in the Legislative Assembly in 1921 for a cut in the budgets of the project; it had been defeated, with many

Indian representatives, including Sir Jamsetjee Jeejeebhoy, coming out strongly in support of the new capital.

New Delhi was formally inaugurated on 10 February 1931, with a ceremony held between the two Secretariat blocks. It involved the unveiling of four pillars, the 'Columns of Dominion', presented to the capital by the four countries in the British Commonwealth which enjoyed 'dominion status'—Canada, South Africa, Australia and New Zealand. Representatives from each of these countries attended the ceremony, except New Zealand, which had a few days ago been struck by a devastating earthquake. Among the crowd of invitees were two—Baker and Alexander Rouse, one of the principal government engineers—who were formally presented as 'the real makers of New Delhi'. Also present among them was Hardinge, referred to by many as 'the father of New Delhi'.

The Times, London, ended its report on the proceedings with the remark that 'it would be idle to pretend that the ceremony had any popular support. The attendance was confined entirely to those admitted by official invitation. All approaches to New Delhi were plastered with armed police, and little encouragement was given to anyone who desired to offer a demonstration, friendly or otherwise.' The Indian press was even more critical. The *Hindustan Times* editorial of 13 February remarked, 'The whole ethos of the proceedings was imperialistic and gave one the impression of having been designed to demonstrate the supremacy of the White Man.'

The following day, events were held that were more inclusive, in the form of a 'People's Fete', in and around Red

Fort. Lord and Lady Irwin sat in the window known as the jharokha-e-darshan, where the British monarch had sat nearly twenty years ago, and the Mughal emperors much before that. Massed bands played in the courtyard of the Diwan-e-Aam in the Red Fort, where the Mughal emperors had once held durbars or assemblies. The crowds watched dances and equestrian events such as tent-pegging competitions and trick riding. The climax was an illuminated fly-past by the Royal Air Force, and a fireworks display.

On 12 February, the All-India War Memorial (India Gate) was dedicated in the memory of India's soldiers who were killed in the war. While Baker had been one of the stars of the event which had taken place during the ceremony at the Secretariat, Lutyens was formally presented at this ceremony, inaugurating one of his important structures. The arch commemorated the more than 70,000 Indian soldiers who had died during World War I. The two fountains, one on either side, as well as the names on the arch, formed a separate memorial—to those soldiers, 12,126 Indian and 1,390 British, who had fallen on the North-West Frontier between 1914-18 and in the third Afghan War of 1919. The tribute ended with the sounding of the 'Last Post' and the lighting of the 'Eternal Flame' at the summit of the arch.

The name chosen for the new capital was New Delhi. It had taken many years to finally arrive at this in late 1926. Various alternatives that had been considered along the way had included Imperial Delhi, Raisina and Delhi South. One suggestion that found its way to Hardinge's desk in 1913, made a pertinent point about the name of the new capital at Delhi. The writer, an Englishman who had served many years in India, pointed out that though the British mostly spelt and pronounced the name as Delhi, this was incorrect. In fact, the name of the place was Dilli or Dehli. He, therefore, proposed that the final name should be one of these. After a brief discussion with Hailey, Hardinge decided that though indeed Delhi was the wrong spelling and pronunciation, long usage by the British had sanctified it. Moreover, it was impossible to choose between Dilli and Dehli!

When the idea of a new capital had been first considered, no one could have anticipated the journey it would take to the inauguration. It had cost, including the purchase of land, over ten-and-a-half million pounds, much over the early official statements that had envisaged an expenditure of less than five million. An average of twenty thousand labourers, including 5,700 skilled workers, had been employed. Some 3,500 had been employed at the stone yard alone, where three-and-a-half million cubic feet of stone had been cut. Seven hundred million bricks had been made in twenty-seven kilns scattered through the area south of the site. Fifty miles of main roads and thirty miles of service roads were constructed.

Various individuals had played important parts in the creation of the city. Hardinge, Swinton, Brodie, Luytens, Baker and Lanchester had all played crucial roles. The government architects, W.H. Nicholls, Montagu Thomas and Robert Tor Russell, had designed many of the buildings in what would erroneously come to be called 'the Lutyens' Bungalow Zone'. Government engineers Hugh Keeling and Alexander Rouse, had the logistical responsibility to organize materials, equipment, and transport. Finally, the work of organizing the labour was executed through several independent contractors—Haroun al Rashid for Government House, Baishakha Singh for North Block and various bungalows, Lachman Das for the Council House, Akbar Ali for the Records Office, Nawab Ali for Mughal Garden, Sujan Singh and his son Sobha Singh for South Block and the Great Place, as well as for several of the states' houses, and Narain Singh for the roads and many of the bungalows. The construction work was carried out by thousands of labourers, known in official parlance as 'coolies', mainly from Rajasthan and Punjab. They were housed in 'coolie lines', on the fringes of the core New Delhi area, for example, at Malcha (west of Government House) Kushak (close to Teen Murti Bhawan), and south of Purana Qila.

New Delhi, unveiled, was a city quite unlike any other. Immediately striking was its Central Vista—King's Way flanked by rows of large trees and wide strips of grass in which lay long ornamental pools of water. The city's most monumental buildings lay along this majestic avenue, terminated at one end by the War Memorial Arch, and at the other by Viceroy's House. Both these structures were the creations of Edwin Lutyens, and invited both popular and professional praise.

Lutyens had struggled to reconcile his own tastes with the requirements of his clients. He was personally inclined to a style inspired by the work of the sixteenth-century Venetian architect Andrea Palladio's interpretation of the classical temple architecture of the ancient Greeks and Romans. His clients, primarily Hardinge, and George V, were equally firmly committed to the introduction of an emphatically Indian style into the architecture of the new imperial capital. One point that led to prolonged discussion was the question of the shape of the arches to be used. Indian architecture had for centuries used pointed arches, but both Lutyens and Baker wanted to use the classical round 'Roman' arch, and this was a point on which they felt strongly. Finally, it was the round arch that was used in the buildings of New Delhi.

Lutyens resolved the conflict between the wishes of his clients and his own professional integrity with considerable creativity. In the form and ornament of Viceroy's House, European and Indian architecture and motifs were blended in a way that did not appear forced. The large dome of the building was modelled on the ancient Buddhist Sanchi Stupa,

Viceroy's House, now Rashtrapati Bhavan

with its flattened summit, and stone railings encircling the deep drum. The dome was unusually high, towering over the rest of the building. Though lime mortar had been used in the construction of all the buildings, for the foundations of the dome the engineers had suggested the use of Portland cement instead, to take the weight of the structure on top.

The drum and the roofline below the dome had additional features that were Indian, but unusually executed. Lutyens had more than once expressed his impatience with chhatris—Indian cupolas supported on pillars, on one occasion calling them 'stupid, useless things.' When called upon to use them nevertheless, he did so innovatively; thus the chhatris around the dome were built close to the drum, barely breaking its silhouette. Those along the parapet were pushed down into it, so as not to break the roofline too abruptly. On the rooftop were water fountains shaped like saucers, reminiscent of Mughal architecture, which had incorporated water channels and pools in buildings as well as gardens. Below the parapet was a deep chhajja or overhanging cornice, an important feature for the provision of shade in Indian buildings. Its installation during 1926-27 had been beset with technical difficulties.

In contrast to these Indian forms, the long colonnade with its tall columns, which made up the facade of the building, was strictly Western in its form. Each pillar was surmounted by a capital in an unusual style—encased with abstract acanthus leaves, with four bells at the corners. This style of pillar capital was specially designed by Lutyens, and is known as the 'Delhi Order'—after the Classical Greek

Orders—Doric, Ionic and Corinthian. This capital was used in several other structures designed by Lutyens for New Delhi—such as the canopy that would be built later near the War Memorial Arch, and the Record Office.

Though the overall finish of the building was restrained, decorative touches were added through carvings of mainly Indian motifs—such as the jalis, or pierced stone screens, modelled on those found in Mughal architecture, and massive basement piers inspired by cave temples. Figures of elephants, snakes, lions and eagles, a mix of Indian and British imagery, were used throughout the complex. Even the material used for cladding, red and buff sandstone, was in harmony with the materials that had been used in the monumental architecture of Delhi for centuries, that is, red sandstone and white marble.

In front of Viceroy's House stood a tall pillar—the Jaipur Column. Its name was a tribute to its donor, the Maharaja of Jaipur, Madho Singh. As the design of Government House was being finalized, Madho Singh had expressed a desire to defray the cost of a memorial pillar which Lutyens intended to set up in the forecourt. This, he said, would be 'a mark of sincere loyalty to the Throne and in remembrance of the gracious courtesy and the many favours I received at the hands of my beloved Sovereign.' This offer was gratefully accepted, and he was informed that the cost of the column would be within two lakhs of rupees.

The design for the column had been worked out by Lutyens by mid-1915. This was approved of by Hardinge, with a couple of reservations. One regarding the petals of

Jaipur Column; photograph from 1948

the lotus which seemed too blunt, was quickly modified by Lutyens. The other was regarding the star at the top, which Lutyens had designed as a three-dimensional six-pointed star, but which from every direction looked like a cross, that is, with four points. Hardinge was apprehensive that this would not be liked by Muslims, and that it was better to have a five-pointed star instead. To this criticism, Lutyens replied that he had actually made a five-pointed star, with one additional 'leg' with which to attach it to the column!

There were other gifts from Indian rulers adorning the exterior of Government House. Two seven-and-a-half-feet tall statues, one of George V by B. Mackennal, and the other of Queen Mary by George Frampton, stood between the columns flanking the portico. These had been planned a long time ago, during the Durbar of 1911. Maharaja Scindia had expressed a desire to erect a statue of George V in the new capital, and this had been announced during the stone laying ceremony. The announcement had prompted the Maharajas of Bikaner, Kapurthala, Alwar and Patiala, separately to write to the Viceroy, saying that they would like to present a statue of Queen Mary, to go with it. It was finally settled that the two statues in coronation robes would be paid for by Maharaja Scindia and the Maharajah of Bikaner respectively, and be sculpted according to the wishes of the King and Queen. There was some discussion about whether they should be in white marble or bronze, and ultimately, the former material was settled on. Hardinge's reasoning was that marble statues would look 'splendid' under a bright sun. Both maharajas acquiesced, Scindia with a simple remark that he was happy to go along with whatever was thought suitable. On the other hand, Ganga Singh of Bikaner explained that his preference was marble mainly 'because in bronze the face, and indeed the whole statue, looks *dark*.'

The interior of Viceroy House had also been carefully worked out. Before the house had even begun to be built, a special advisory body, designated 'The Home Committee on the Furnishing and Decoration of Government House', was appointed in London, at the instance of Crewe, with advice from Lutyens. It held its first meeting on 1 December 1914 before Lutyens left for India once again. One of its provisional decisions was to use a style of furnishing that would be completely Western, preferably English, with a spare use of Indian, Persian and Chinese motifs. The setting up of the committee, in faraway London, was not without its complications. Hardinge seems to have felt that its dictating matters regarding the interiors of Government House was not appropriate. In February 1916, he declared, 'I do not wish to have anything to say or do with the self-constituted Committee in London for the Furnishing of Government House, as I disapprove entirely of their meddlesome interference.'

Lutyens found that the task of furnishing Government House became easy after the arrival of Irwin as Viceroy in 1926. The new Viceroy and Lady Irwin were great supporters and admirers of his designs, and as a consequence, allowed him a free rein in ordering material, both in India and abroad. He eventually designed almost every detail of the interiors. The execution of the furniture and furnishings was worked out with the help of an expert from England, who was called in 'to advise on the manner in which the resources of the country could be worked up to the highest European standards'. According to the PWD report, for the construction of the furniture 'a kiln to season timber by steam was under construction from England'. The use of steam for seasoning was considered appropriate to allow for the humidity of the monsoon which the finished pieces would have to withstand. PWD engineers often complained that Lutyens' perfectionism concerning the quality of the finish was also leading to delays. There were disagreements because Lutyens insisted on superior materials, for instance, when 'progress on the sanitary schemes was slow owing to the difficulty experienced in meeting the Architect's wishes with regards to the type of fittings to be used.'

Lutyens had devised schemes of mural decoration for

some of the state rooms in Government House. For Durbar Hall he had proposed a depiction of 'a procession of India's great men with outstanding events in India's history shown in the several panels and cartouches.' This was eventually not executed. The Council Room (now called the Cabinet Room) did, however, get an elaborate scheme of pictorial maps, showing international routes of communication, decorating the upper parts of its walls. The work was carried out by a team of artists headed by Munshi Ghulam Hussain. Percy Brown, then principal of the Government School of Art at Calcutta, had supervised the work, and recommended Ghulam Hussain for the title of Khan Bahadur, for his lifelong work as an artist. An elaborate set of ceiling paintings in the Ballroom (today called Ashoka Hall), in a traditional Persian style, were commissioned later, in 1932-33.

Immediately behind Viceroy's House lay a formal garden, modelled on the Mughal charbaghs—formal gardens on a fourfold grid of parterres, water channels and walkways. Early in the process of the designing of Government House, Hardinge had received some valuable suggestions regarding the gardens from Constance Villiers-Stuart, who had worked on a study of traditional Indian, particularly Mughal, gardens. She suggested the suitability of an enclosed garden with no drives or roads, just pathways and waterways. Though at the time Hardinge did not commit himself, being of the view that the details of the garden would be worked out under his successor, the idea was passed on to Lutyens. The latter wrote to his wife in 1917, 'I submitted my plan for the gardens of Government House. They—the Government of

India—commanded a Mogul garden which means terraces, waterways, sunk courts, high walls, etc. etc...It is too Alice in Wonderlandish for words.' Sarojini Naidu had even suggested a name for the garden to Villiers-Stuart—'Garden of Unity'. This, however, was never adopted, and it came to be known simply as the Mughal Garden.

The Secretariat buildings were as impressive as Government House. They rose up majestically from the Great Place, forming the 'stupendous platform' Baker had aimed for. This effect was amply achieved, as Indians soon began to call the Secretariat 'Raisina ka qila' or the 'Fort of Raisina'. Here the Indian elements were more obvious, and blended less subtly with the classical Western ones than in Lutyens' architecture. Chhatris, jalis and carved brackets supporting decorative balconies, were clearly in evidence, next to Renaissance-style domes and classical columns. Elephant heads carved on domes and pillars carried the Indian theme forward, though large life-sized elephants that had been planned for the base of the Secretariat blocks were never built. An inscription on the entrance to the North Block proclaimed: 'Liberty will not descend to a people. A people must raise themselves to liberty. It is a blessing that must be earned before it can be enjoyed.' If this was a response to the rising national movement, it was a patronizing and offensive one.

A series of wall paintings decorated seven rooms inside the Secretariat blocks. Of interest was a large, elaborate frieze in the Law Members' Chamber in North Block, executed by M.V. Dhurandhar of the JJ School of Art, Bombay, which depicted the British legal system at work in India, evenly dispensing justice according to the traditional laws of Hindus and Muslims. Another, in the Princes' Waiting Room in South Block, depicted the four varnas, Brahman, Kshatriya, Vaishya and Shudra, painted by G.H. Nagarkar, also of the JJ School of Art.

Somewhat at a distance, to the east of the North Block of the Secretariat, lay Council House. This was, to some observers at least, a disappointment. Robert Byron, writing for *Architectural Review*, compared the thin pillars making up its colonnade to 'the iron struts of a fender'. An attic storey for the building had been added as an afterthought in 1928-29, and had obscured the central dome, which now appeared as 'an irrelevant wart-like cupola'. The best that could be said about it was that 'its unobtrusiveness is a major virtue'.

At the other end of the Central Vista lay Princes' Park, a hexagonal island of green around which were grouped the houses of the various 'princes'. A total of thirty-six states were allotted plots in New Delhi, ranging in size from three to nine acres. Design controls had been laid down so that there would be some amount of harmony with regard to placement of boundaries and gates on the sites, as well as with the architectural style of New Delhi. Lutyens himself was the architect of Hyderabad and Baroda Houses, and several others followed the style fairly closely. Of the palaces, Hyderabad and Bikaner Houses were the first to be completed, in 1928. When the capital was inaugurated in 1931, there had been little further activity on sites allotted to princely states, with the exception of Baroda House and

Travancore House, which were under construction. The Maharaja of Kashmir had not built but purchased a house in 1928—one that had been recently built as the residence of the Commander-in-Chief on King George's Avenue (now Rajaji Marg). A new residence was subsequently built for the latter, south of Viceroy's House.

A visitor to New Delhi, looking at its newly built splendours, particularly the grand Central Vista, mused, 'What is the exact significance of this little Versailles Delhiesque? What does this heap of stones, this orgy of colonnades, mean? Why those colossal avenues, these bare Champs Elysees, these over-large fountains, these dazzling lights?...Whatever one's opinion may be of the aesthetic value of these palaces, one cannot help trying to discover the significance of this monumental display. One ends up by finding it in the necessity to impress upon Indians, from the millionaire potentate to the starving sweeper, a respect for British power.'

For a city that had its roots in a desire to ensure more Indian participation in the empire, there was much that was wrong with this message, as well as with the exclusive nature of the inauguration ceremony. What had gone wrong? Beginning with the Coronation Durbar of 1911, the entire project had been heavy on symbolism. Indians were invited to imagine George V as their ruler because he appeared to them in the jharokha-e-darshan, just as the Mughal emperors once had; and to believe that the British Indian empire was in the lineage of Indian empires simply because its new capital very literally lined up with the Indraprastha of the Pandavas

India Gate: a photograph from 26 January 1950

and Shahjahanabad of the Mughals. The superficially 'Indian' features of the public buildings of New Delhi were meant to convince Indians that those who worked within them, worked for the benefit of the Indian people.

The problem was that these grand gestures were not backed up by any substantial change on the ground. Growing public opinion in India was questioning an empire that ruled India for the benefit of a home population in Britain. Just one week after the inauguration, Mahatma Gandhi, recently released from prison, entered Viceroy's House for discussions with Irwin, to work out a truce to enable further talks on constitutional reform. This meeting was a controversial one. The idea of a compromise was unpalatable to many in Britain. Conservative Member of Parliament, Winston Churchill, remarked, 'It is alarming and also nauseating to see Mr Gandhi, a seditious Middle Temple lawyer, now posing as a fakir of a type well known in the East, striding half-naked up the steps of the Viceregal palace...to parley on equal terms with the representative of the King-Emperor.' The Viceroy's House, in his opinion, was the seat of the representative of the British monarch, where a leader of the Indian people had no place.

Nor were the compromises offered by the resulting Gandhi-Irwin Pact, a temporary truce which paved the way for Congress participation in the Second Round Table conference in London, acceptable in the long run to the Indian leadership. By the end of the year, the Civil Disobedience Movement had been resumed, and Gandhi as well as many hundred Congress leaders were in jail.

When it was conceived of in 1911, the idea of the new capital held the promise of a renewed empire, one that would enjoy the support of Indian subjects. At its inauguration nearly two decades later, not only had that promise not been lived up to, faith in the vision itself, that it was possible to have an empire which worked with and for its Indian subjects, had faded. All that was left was a grandeur that signified the profound inequality of colonial relationships.

Plaza Cinema; a photograph of 1953

Connaught Place: Life of the City

WHILE THE CENTRAL VISTA AND THE GOVERNMENT BUILDINGS were definitely impressive, it was the commercial centre that gave life to the city. Soon after the intention to build a new capital in Delhi had been announced, calls for a distinct shopping centre to be established in Delhi had come, mainly from representatives of the European commercial community of Calcutta. It was suggested that the 'Government should in the new city apportionate a part for a shopping centre or district on one of the main roads or "Mall". So that anyone shopping can get all their requirements in one centre'. Firms had also begun to request that sites be allotted to them at reasonable rates, promising that they would put up 'suitable buildings worthy of the New Imperial Delhi'. The suggestions and requests received a positive response from the government.

The Town Planning Committee, in its report of 1913, had earmarked for this purpose an area towards the north of the city, the apex of a triangle which had Government House and Princes' Park as its two other corners. The layout of this commercial precinct was envisaged as a circle, with the central portion being occupied by a dominant railway terminus. Administrative and municipal offices, the post office, shops and hotels would be grouped in front of this railway station. This idea, however, was abandoned in early 1914, on the grounds of expense, and the station was built further north. The plaza, therefore, became a predominantly commercial centre. The buildings were constructed with private investment, and blocks were sold individually. At the same time, it was decided that in order to ensure that there was architectural harmony and dignity, the complex would be designed in the form of a unified whole, by the government architects—in effect, the architect member of the Imperial Delhi Committee. A preliminary design for the large circle of blocks was conceived by Nicholls, and detailed plans were completed by his successor, Russell.

The design was clearly inspired by majestic crescents, such as Park Crescent in London and The Circus in the town of Bath, though many would criticise the plan for not being as imposing. The buildings were laid in the pattern of an incomplete circle, or as some called it, a horseshoe, consisting of two concentric rings of double-storeyed blocks. In 1927

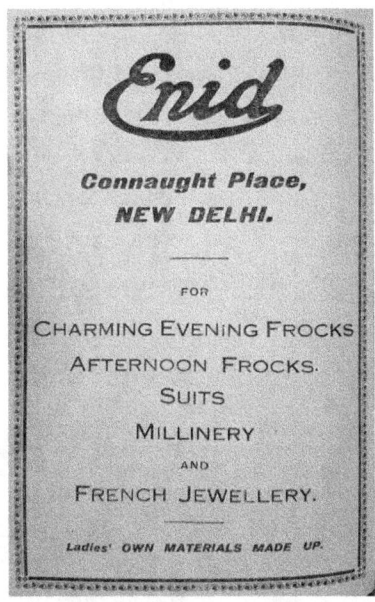

From the New Delhi Directory 1929-30

the complex was named after Edward VII's brother, Lord Arthur, the Duke of Connaught, with the inner circle being named Connaught Place, and the outer circle, Connaught Circus. The open area within the inner circle was covered by expansive lawns, and in the centre was a bandstand, a hallmark of many British colonial stations in India. Here band music was played every Saturday from the middle of October to mid-April, the duration of the Delhi 'season', when officialdom descended from the summer sojourn in Simla. Under the bandstand, and not normally visible to casual observers, was housed an electric storage and distribution station.

Connaught Place was built on a generous and open scale, much like New Delhi as a whole. Unlike compact cities like the Mughal Shahjahanabad, this was urban design meant for the age of motorized transport. Though the elite who patronized it often had motor cars, others who wished to visit from neighbouring Old Delhi or from other parts of New Delhi itself were dependent on horse-drawn tongas or a very limited bus service which ran along the Circus. By way of additional public transport, a trolley bus service, consisting of buses drawing power from overhead electric lines, was introduced in 1934 and ran for a couple of decades, linking Civil Lines via Old Delhi to Connaught Place.

Progress on building the complex was dependent on investors coming forward, and this began to pick up pace only in the 1920s. Blocks were built at an uneven rate, consistent only with when and where places were sold. Half of the premises set aside for commercial spaces in the inner circle had been disposed of by 1926, and work had begun on one of the blocks. By the following year, all the premises in the inner ring had been taken up, and construction work on two large blocks was progressing fast. Tenants moved into shops in two of the large blocks in 1927-28, and in 1929-30, three more blocks were constructed.

The ten blocks of the outer ring, Connaught Circus, included the buildings of large offices and institutions, such as the *Statesman* newspaper, and the Burmah Shell Oil Company. Also in this location was Scindia House, originally bought by the Maharaja of Gwalior, who intended it to be office space for Scindia Potteries. Soon after, however, he had second thoughts about the soundness of the investment and sold it to Sobha Singh, one of the contractors of New Delhi, who had made many other investments in property around the capital. The name, 'Scindia House', which had already been entered into various documents, continued.

Another of Sobha Singh's investments in Connaught Place was a building for a theatre on a 3.44 acre site. Plans were approved in 1930, and it was noted that the lessee proposed

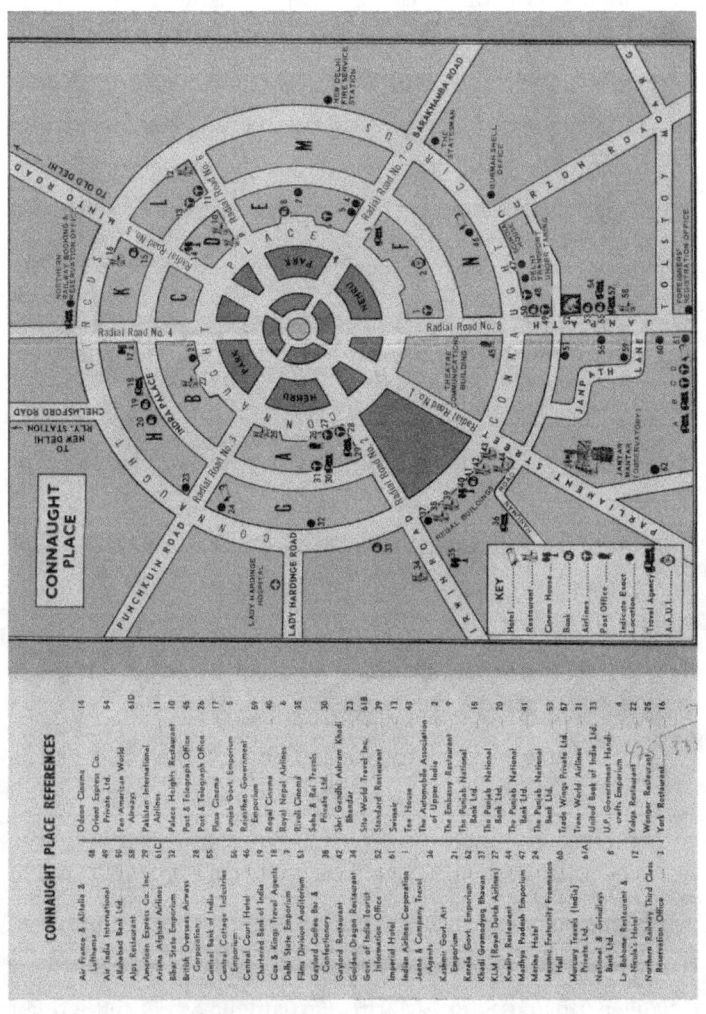

Connaught Place; from a guide map of 1961

to 'equip the site with a spacious and elaborate building at an estimated cost of six lakhs of rupees, which will provide besides the theatre, a cinema and a Rink Hall with gardens, shops, etc'. The theatre building was completed in 1932 and came to be famous as Regal, a theatre that staged plays as well as screened films, and was managed by Sobha Singh himself. It aimed to attract an upmarket clientele with its six exclusive boxes and its bar. The building also housed high-end shops and restaurants.

Other movie theatres were built soon after. Plaza in 1933, Odeon in 1940 and Rivoli in 1941. While these halls mostly screened English language films, one theatre was specifically opened for Indian films. This was the Raisina Theatre, on Irwin Road (Baba Kharak Singh Marg), set up in 1938 by the Seth brothers. Interestingly, there was at least one, probably temporary, cinema that predated these theatres. In the Delhi Directory of 1929-30, we find listed the Prince of Wales Cinema in Talkatora Garden. The garden was a historic place, located north of the Viceregal Estate.

The commercial spread reached beyond the main blocks of Connaught Place, into nearby areas too. Gole Market, constructed in the early 1920s by the government, was the first market to be built in New Delhi. In 1928-29, a private firm built a row of shops nearby, at the junction of Baird Road (Bangla Sahib Road) and Lady Hardinge Road (Shaheed Bhagat Singh Marg). Parliament Street, which lay off Connaught Place, was on the other hand characterized more by institutions and offices. Interestingly, it was known as 'Parliament Street' even in the 1920s, though the building

From the New Delhi Directory
1929-30

after which it was named, was still called Council House. This important road was to see the construction of several institutional buildings. The Imperial Bank of India opened a branch here on 1 January 1926, and Reuters moved into its new building on this road in 1928. Two large blocks of flats, facing each other, were also built on this street. Broadcasting House, housing the studios of All India Radio, was built later, in 1943.

Narain Singh, another of the contractors for the New Delhi construction, had invested in a plot of land just under eight acres, on Queen's Way. Here, he and his son Ranjit Singh, built New Delhi's first large hotel, the Imperial, which opened in 1936. Designed in an Art Deco style by the architects C.G. and F.B. Blomfield, it was a departure from both the Lutyenesque style evident in the Central Vista, and the Neo-Classical of Connaught Place. The interiors were lavishly furnished, with the best materials from around the world. The Vicerene, Lady Willingdon, had reportedly taken a personal interest, picking materials at the leading shops in London.

A guidebook of the early 1940s described Connaught Place as 'indeed the most fashionable shopping centre of and the most crowded spot in New Delhi, the stronghold of leading business houses, the seat of prominent social institutions, and what is more, undoubtedly the most progressive part of the most progressive town in the country'. In fact, the businesses that opened in the newly built Connaught Place and its neighbouring commercial areas, mostly catered to the elite of the new capital. Many of the retail businesses that moved into Connaught Place were institutions that already had a presence in other British enclaves, such as Calcutta or Simla, or in Delhi itself—in Kashmiri Gate, which was a fashionable shopping area catering to the nearby Civil Lines.

Cooke & Kelvey, specializing in luxury watches and jewellery, were from Calcutta. Indian Arts Palace, which had been selling gems, jewellery and antiques from outlets in

Connaught Place in 1946

Chandni Chowk and Kashmiri Gate, opened in Connaught Place in 1935. Fashionable clothiers seem to have been especially in demand and several purveyors set themselves up in Connaught Place. B. Lilaram and Son, silk merchants, tailors and outfitters, were proud to announce themselves 'by appointment to' the Viceroy and the Commander-in-Chief, with branches in several towns in North India. Originally located in Kashmiri Gate, they soon opened in Connaught Place. Enid specialized in women's frocks, hats and 'French jewellery', and G.R. Parker in shirt-making and men's formal wear. Another tailoring and outfitting establishment, Raghbir Singh, catered to both male and female clients. To complete the appearance of the fashionable set, the Royal Hairdressing Salon employed a 'qualified London trained hair dresser' and claimed to be 'patronized by Lords and Maharajas'. The Army and Navy Store, specializing in household goods as well as clothes, was housed in Regal Building. A new tailoring establishment, Vaish, opened in the Rivoli Cinema building in 1939. A lower rung of somewhat less elite tailoring establishments came up on Panchkuian Road.

Also answering to the needs of the mostly British elite was a clutch of food businesses. Some of these were high-end grocers, catering specifically to European culinary tastes. They included stores like Sarab Dayal & Co, general merchants, who specially advertised their Dutch, Cheddar and Gruyere cheese, cigars, and chocolates; and J Morton & Co, 'For your High Class Wines, Provisions, Cigars and Cigarettes'. Keventers, who ran a dairy farm in the city (in present-day Chanakyapuri, just off Mother Teresa Crescent), opened an outlet for dairy products. On the other hand, shops for produce such as poultry and fish, and a wide variety of grocers, were located in Gole Market rather than Connaught Place, presumably because it was not the sahibs and memsahibs themselves, but their domestic staff, who shopped for these daily essentials. After all, as one visitor remarked, Connaught Place was where elegant ladies shopped, wearing hats and gloves.

The food business also included catering services, confectioners and restaurants. Often these three functions were undertaken by the same establishment, such as Davico Ltd., which proudly proclaimed that it was by appointment to the Viceroy. With its initial base in Kashmiri Gate, it soon opened a restaurant in Connaught Place for lunch, tea and dinner. A special attraction of Davico's was the orchestra that accompanied the 'tea dances' every Thursday and Saturday. A similar establishment was Wenger & Co, which had originally been in Kashmiri Gate where it functioned under the name of Spencer's. It was set up by a Swiss couple, who later sold the business to B.M. Tandon, in 1945. Its premises in A Block of Connaught Place had a distinctly European ambience, with high ceilings and columns in the bakery's ground floor lobby. The first floor had a spacious ballroom, a café and a restaurant with open verandahs. A third confectioner-cum-caterer-cum-restaurant, though not as well-known as these two in Connaught Place, was the Italian, Carlo Pezza, in Baird Road (now Bangla Sahib Road).

Other shops and services appeared quite quickly in

Connaught Place. There were bookshops such as E.D. Galgotia and Sons, newsagents and booksellers, Amrit Book Company and the English Book Depot. Ram Chandra Jain, who owned a printing press in Old Delhi, started Connaught Place's first art gallery, Dhoomi Mal's, in 1936 from a shop that sold stationery and art materials. In 1935, Ram Chander & Son's, a toy shop with its headquarters in Ambala cantonment, opened in Block D of Connaught Place.

One of the earliest doctors to be listed in Connaught Place was S.M. Elahie, dentist. In nearby Baird Road, Dr Kriparam & Sons advertised themselves as 'chemists, opticians and photo goods dealers'. In the 1920s and '30s it seems to have been usual for chemists to stock photographic goods, as we can see from the profile of Chhajju Ram and Sons, also on Baird Road, and Plomer and Co in Connaught Place. Baird Road was also home to New Capital Cycle Store, which, in addition to selling cycles, provided the service of storing them during the summer season, when owners departed for Simla.

In a city where many construction projects were on through these decades, architects and building contractors formed an important component of service providers. Several of these set up offices in Connaught Place or Jantar Mantar Road. The architects C.G. and F.B. Blomfield (who had designed Bikaner House and Jaipur House), and Walter Sykes George (best known for his design of St Stephen's College in the North Campus of the University, and the St Martin's Church in the cantonment, but who also designed Regal Cinema, Ambassador Hotel and Sujan Singh Park), who had worked initially on government buildings, had set up flourishing private practices and had offices in Connaught Place. Other services associated with the construction trade also established outlets. In Connaught Place, Bhagwan Singh and Sons stocked electrical goods and undertook electrical jobs. In nearby Panchkuian Road were other suppliers of electrical services, and furniture makers.

Despite the elegant shops, restaurants and cinemas, Connaught Place was a relatively quiet place in its early years, genteel rather than lively. Moreover, its main clientele—the upper bureaucracy and the other well-heeled members of society, disappeared to Simla for long periods in the summer. This was inimical to good business, except for a few of the establishments that had parallel outlets in the summer capital. Things changed in the 1940s, with the outbreak of World War II, particularly when Delhi became the supply hub of the war in the Pacific. For one, the official population of Delhi increased. There was an overall increase in officials due to the expansion and addition of government departments to deal with the new functions related to the war. Also, many more officials began to stay behind in Delhi during the summer, and by 1942 the annual exodus to Simla in the summer ended altogether.

Apart from government officials, there was an influx of other categories of people—members of new diplomatic missions which were being established in the city, journalists from all over the world, and the personnel of Britain's wartime allies, mainly Americans, who were stationed in Delhi. The increase in numbers, as well as a somewhat greater diversity in

Republic Day Parade through Connaught Place in 1962

social life, brought the city, and particularly Connaught Place, alive during the wartime years. In particular, the presence of a large number of well-paid American soldiers and officials, led to increased business for the shops, restaurants, cinemas, taxis and tongas. Americans were also more informal, and often struck up easy friendships with the non-official population. Indeed it was remarked that their 'uninhibited ways' eroded 'the city's carefully cultivated imperial ambience'.

Entrepreneurs were quick to take advantage of the new opportunities. The two Nirula brothers, who ran a photo studio in D Block, had opened Hotel India in the same block in 1934. In 1942 they took on rent large ground floor premises in L Block, which, for lack of tenants, was being used for storing charpais (string cots). Here they opened a restaurant and bar called Nirula's Corner House. Its attractions were more exciting than those of the older restaurants. The entertainment included cabaret, flamenco dancers, magicians and ballroom dancing, clearly looking for patronage beyond the straitlaced official class. For food, it served Indian as well as 'Continental' cuisine, testament to the more eclectic clientele it attracted—Indians, but also Americans and others keen to experiment with unfamiliar cuisines.

The Nirulas were old Delhi inhabitants, but newcomers too succeeded. One was Pishori Lal Lamba, who arrived in Delhi from Lahore in 1940. His handmade ice-cream store, Kwality's, which he set up with his business partner Iqbal Ghai, was a huge hit, particularly with the American soldiers. It was reportedly advice from a US army veterinary surgeon that led him to embark on the commercial ice-cream business, which gave birth to one of India's most successful brands.

By the end of the war, Connaught Place had become established, was bustling with many flourishing businesses and a reasonably diverse, though still fairly elite, clientele. Many of the shops, restaurants and cinemas that were set up then, would last into the twenty-first century.

Gole Dak Khana, the post office

The Contours of Civic Life

THE NEW DELHI THAT WAS INAUGURATED IN 1931, DIFFERED in some important details from the plan that had been submitted by the Town Planning Committee in 1913. Most of these departures from the original scheme were due to financial constraints, as those projects that were not considered essential, were dropped. There were other reasons too, including the changed political climate of the post-World War I period.

One cut in expenditure had been achieved by indefinitely postponing the construction of those public buildings that were not immediately necessary. In 1928, the building of the Record Office (what is now known as the National Archives of India) had been completed at an exorbitant cost of fifteen lakh rupees. The record office was located on the northwest side of the junction between King's Way and Queen's Way. It was designed by Lutyens, and covered in red and buff sandstone like the other principal government buildings. The original plan envisaged three other similar buildings, making up an 'ethnological museum', including a Central Asian Museum, one on each of the remaining quadrants of the crossing. While the full plan was put on hold, for a while the idea of building at least one of them, on the opposite side of King's Way, was considered. As a measure of economy, it was suggested that instead of the stone facing, the building be finished in plaster, which would result in a saving of six lakhs. This too was never implemented, and the construction of the museum had to wait till after Independence. The National Museum was eventually built, on a plot of land a little further away, between 1955 and 1960.

The original scheme of the Town Planning Committee had made provision for a 'durbar amphitheatre,' a venue for future durbars, located at the base of the Ridge, west of Government House. It remained indefinitely in abeyance, mainly because of the huge expense that would be involved. Eventually it was decided that instead, a suitable venue would be 'the sunk gardens at the east end of the Central Vista... (where) a nucleus of permanent buildings would always be useful for various annual functions such as Birthday (of the British monarch) and Proclamation (of coronations) parades, reviews of troops, horse shows, hockey and football tournaments, etc.' This suggestion, approved of by Lutyens, was the genesis of the Irwin Amphitheatre, built in 1933. This was later renamed National Stadium, and is today Major Dhyan Chand Stadium.

The reason why the stadium could be built in this location, between Purana Qila and Princes' Park, was because the original idea, of creating a lake in that location, had been abandoned. In its report, the Town Planning Committee had suggested an elaborate plan to bring the Yamuna more or less back to its old course beside the three historic cities of Delhi that once lay on its bank—Shahjahanabad, Ferozabad, and Dinpanah (Purana Qila). It had, in 1913, roughly estimated that this would cost around 250,000 pounds sterling. This, at a time when the figures for the capital project were being estimated in the neighbourhood of five million pounds, was a considerable outlay. Since the benefit would have been more aesthetic than utilitarian, the project was never implemented. This led to a situation where, in the words of the writer Nirad Chaudhuri, 'the city was totally separated from the river on which it stood, and made to turn its back on it...Standing on the bank of the Jumna, nobody could suspect that the capital of India was behind him, and when in the city no one could guess that it was on a famous river'.

Another part of the scheme that was not fully implemented was the improvement of the old city, and its connection at various points with the new city through new roads. The idea of connecting the new capital to the old Mughal one, Shahjahanabad, had been debated from an early date. The early thoughts of the Town Planning Committee, to align the main avenue of the new city with the Jama Masjid, had presumed a physical link between the two cities. Hand in hand with this scheme went projects for the 'improvement' of the old city, in terms of sanitation, health and aesthetics. Even after it had been decided that the suburb of Paharganj, which lay between the old and new cities, could not be cleared, the question of linking the two areas remained an important part of the plan.

In a seeming contradiction, early plans, while they spoke of important physical links between Shahjahanabad and New Delhi, also envisaged a *cordon sanitaire*, literally a 'sanitary buffer', between the two. This took the form of a green strip of land, euphemistically named 'People's Park', along one side of which ran the stone city wall of Shahjahanabad, serving as a picturesque backdrop, as well as a curtain to hide the overcrowding and squalor which, officials were convinced, lay behind it. The contradiction arose from conflicting goals. A ceremonial axis from Red Fort to New Delhi was seen as a powerful symbolic gesture, the road to St James Church and Civil Lines beyond as a practical necessity for linking Civil Lines, the old European enclave, with the new one. And yet, there was a desire to separate New Delhi from the chaos and unsanitary conditions of Shahjahanabad, which were, incidentally, the result of years of neglect of civic amenities. The solution, as far as the city planners were concerned, lay in 'improving' those areas of Shahjahanabad that would be directly connected to New Delhi, while hiding away and separating those that were not so connected.

As a climate of austerity set in, the value of mere symbolism, that is, the idea of creating a ceremonial avenue from Red Fort to Purana Qila, also declined. It was not just the cost which was a factor in this case. The rising national movement was in evidence in Delhi as much as anywhere else in the country, and Shahjahanabad was seen not only as a hotbed of infection, but of political unrest. At the northern end of the originally proposed ceremonial road, just south of Red Fort, the foundation stone for a King Edward Memorial had already been laid by the departed monarch's son, George V, in 1911. A park was subsequently created here, with an equestrian statue of Edward VII duly installed, but this was the mere completion of an idea that was a leftover from an earlier era. When Edward's brother Arthur, the Duke of Connaught, had visited Delhi in 1921, his passage through Old Delhi had to be secured by troops. In 1929, the Hindustan Socialist Republican Army threw a bomb into the Legislative Assembly and later that year, as the Viceroy's train pulled into King's Way Station in Civil Lines, another bomb was thrown under it. Under such circumstances, the desire to use a ceremonial avenue that went through Old Delhi was not considered wise.

Within New Delhi, one sector of the city plan that worked out very differently, was that of educational institutions. In the early allotment of space, two plots of land, roughly the triangular area bounded by present-day Feroz Shah Road, Barakhamba Road and Janpath, had been set aside for 'educational institutions'. By mid-1915 it had been decided that these institutions would include a university (of which Delhi, at the time, had none) and two colleges (either Hindu College or a proposed government college, and St Stephen's

College). To accommodate these institutions, two adjacent plots of land, south of Feroz Shah Road, were added to this allotment, making a total of 170 acres. Blueprints of proposed buildings were also deliberated upon in late 1915.

The plan to set up a university in Delhi continued to be debated over the next several years. One major stumbling block was the expenditure anticipated—the buildings alone would cost around thirty lakhs. The university was established, in 1922, but the idea of building the expensive facilities in New Delhi was dropped. The land reserved for the university and its colleges was released for other purposes, mostly sold more lucratively as residential plots. The university was eventually housed in a campus north of Shahjahanabad in a variety of existing buildings. The only colleges that were established in New Delhi were Lady Hardinge College and Lady Irwin College, both of which enjoyed a special status, having been set up under the patronage of two Vicerenes.

In the original allotment, plots of land had also been set aside for schools—one for 'children of Indian clerks', one for 'children of European clerks' and one 'girls' school' close to the clerks' quarters in the northwest quadrant of the city. The idea behind the location of several schools in this quarter was that the many clerks employed in government service, for whom quarters were built in this area, would need schools for their children. It was assumed that senior British officials' children invariably went to boarding schools in the hills, or in England.

In the event, several schools were opened. Since many of the Indian clerical employees of the government were

Bengali and Tamil, they applied for land for schools that would cater to the special cultural and educational needs of their children. The Raisina Bengali School and the Delhi Tamil Educational Association School both opened in 1925. The latter (originally the Madrasi Educational Association School) was given land on the Ridge, on Reading Road (now called Mandir Marg). The Raisina Bengali School was also eventually given premises on Reading Road, after having functioned from various locations within New Delhi. This road, in fact, became the address of several schools. In October 1932, a boys' high school (now known as N.P. Boys Senior Secondary School) was opened. Harcourt Butler School, which used to shift seasonally between Simla and Delhi as the Government of India moved between its summer and winter capitals, had its Delhi premises here. Also on this road was St Thomas' School, an Anglican missionary school founded in 1930. Some other denominational schools also opened, at other locations—the Convent of Jesus and Mary in 1923, and St Columba's School in 1941. Some schools which had originally been set up outside the New Delhi area, also moved to New Delhi. For instance, Modern School, which had begun in 1920 in Daryaganj, applied for and was granted land on Barakhamba Road in 1930.

Land was allocated in the new capital for a number of places of worship. In the plan accompanying the final report of the Town Planning Committee, a prominent place had been demarcated for the Anglican Cathedral, at an important junction of roads, now known as Motilal Nehru Place. This never materialized, probably as it was felt that since the

St Columba's School

majority of the British in Delhi were Anglican Christians, this would give the impression of official support to that denomination. Instead, the Anglican Cathedral came up north of the Viceroy's House, and was financed largely by the Christian congregation and not by the government. The foundation stone for the church, which would eventually be called the Cathedral Church of the Redemption, was laid in February 1927.

Other Christian denominations built their churches too. The foundation stone for the Free Church was laid in March 1927 and it was constructed and in use the next year. A site had been leased for a Roman Catholic church, but the building that first came up on a part of it was the Convent of Jesus and Mary School, in 1926-27. The church, built from 1930-35, was designed by Henry Medd, who also designed the Cathedral Church of the Redemption. Medd went on to succeed Russell as Chief Architect to the Government of India. Land was also allotted for Baptist and Methodist churches. A church for 'sweepers' (a telling comment on caste segregation among the Christian community at the time), St Thomas', was designed by Walter Sykes George, and built on Reading Road in 1933.

The number of places of worship that already existed on the land on which New Delhi was built, continued to serve the needs of other religious groups. A prominent addition however was a large temple, the Lakshminarayan Temple, built by the industrialist Baldeo Das Birla. Other religious and non-religious institutions that carried out construction in New Delhi included the Arya Samaj, whose building on Hanuman Road was completed in 1931, the Young Men's Christian Association, which built its facilities in 1927-28, and the Freemasons, who acquired a plot of land for their building on Queen's Way.

In the building of New Delhi, there had been some attempt to control the style and look of the various structures that would be built in it. All government buildings, of course, were directly the handiwork of government-appointed architects, but it had been envisaged that the architect member of the Imperial Delhi Committee would supervise 'the architecture of such buildings as may be erected by private persons'. A conscious decision was made that prominent buildings, in particular, be made to harmonize with the architectural examples set by the Capitol buildings of New Delhi. This was often achieved by the simple expedient of engaging the same architects who had helped design the government buildings. Architects like Henry Medd and Walter Sykes George, who had worked with Lutyens and Baker on the Capitol buildings, carried important influences from that complex into the buildings they designed. The influence was, of course, most evident in the buildings designed by Lutyens himself, such as Hyderabad House and Baroda House, but also in others. Such imitation however was not to everyone's taste; one observer described 'Bahawalpur House as the illegitimate and untouchable offspring of the Viceregal Lodge'.

The vast majority of residential bungalows and flats in Delhi were built for the use of government employees, by the Public Works Department. In time, interest in private residential plots also developed and speeded up after the end of World War I. In February 1922, 102 acres of land, divided into sixty-one residential units, was auctioned, at an average of Rs 3,990 per acre. The number of leases had risen to 152 by December 1923, and 559 acres of land had, by then, been disposed of for a premium of Rs 9,20,100. Nine large sites, bordering on Aurangzeb, Albuqurque, Prithviraj and York Roads, were disposed of by public auction in 1928-29, and building commenced immediately. By this time, indeed, a number of private houses were reported to have been constructed. Houses in Bengali Market were completed by 1938-39, and the following year, a block of private shops was built, to serve the needs of the residents of the new colony.

The increasing pace of construction was accompanied by an increase in population. The 1931 census revealed a population of 73,653 persons, a 95 per cent increase over the figures of 1921. The figure had risen to 93,733 in the 1941 census. This was, however, the count for winter. In summer, the population used to dip sharply, as not only the government and its officials, but even some schools and commercial businesses in Connaught Place used to shut shop and move to Simla.

Civic life in the capital grew rapidly once a sufficient number of residents had moved in. From the time right after the transfer of the capital and the intention to build a new city had been announced, many had seen in it the opening up of opportunities. The secretary of the Tollygunge Club, in Calcutta, wrote on 17 January 1912, asking that his services be considered when it came to setting up a club in Delhi. The club was soon set up, in 1913, as the Imperial Delhi Gymkhana Club, and was registered as a company with two hundred members, mostly high-ranking officials. It functioned both in Delhi and Simla, though initially in Delhi it was located in Civil Lines, the 'temporary capital'. Work on its eventual premises only began in 1928, and it was occupied in 1929. Chelmsford Club also leased land in the new city, though at first it was housed in temporary buildings that had been put up to house the offices of the Chief Engineer, PWD.

Membership of the clubs was based on a class and race hierarchy, which was understood by all. Chelmsford Club 'never acquired the prestige which belonged to the Imperial Gymkhana Club,' since it was the club for 'the Indians who held high appointment in the Government of India',

Gurudwara Rakab Ganj and the Cathedral Church of the Redemption

and 'formed the second tier of the administrative hierarchy socially, however high their official rank might be'. It was no surprise that Hardinge was invited to become Patron of the Gymkhana Club, 'the material symbol of New Delhi life'.

The same social set that frequented the clubs, patronized the Delhi Race Course, which began its operations in 1926-27. Maurice Dekobra, the French writer, visited Delhi soon after the race course became operational, and wrote of the scene tongue-in-cheek: 'Two o'clock. The avenue which leads to the polo grounds at Delhi is thronged with sports cars and Rolls-Royces. Glittering in the sun, the Maharajah of Alwar's car passes. A limousine, whose body is all aluminium, shimmers like a mirror...The buffaloes, when they see this meteor pass, are astonished in spite of everything, and cease chewing the cud for some seconds.' The contrast between the sophistication of the race course and the rural touch provided by the cattle that still roamed the city's streets was stark!

For those who were not part of the upper echelons of society, avenues of entertainment were limited, in contrast to the cultural and social offerings that Old Delhi possessed in abundance. Visits to parks, of which the city contained a number, soon became a popular pastime. The park that had been created around a dense collection of important tombs towards the south of the city, was initially named Lodi Park. It was later officially inaugurated by Lady Willingdon on 9 April 1936, and came to be known as Lady Willingdon Park. The name Lodi Park continued in popular usage, and was revived after Independence as Lodi Garden.

People also liked to visit the newly spruced up historical

sites—Humayun's Tomb, Safdarjung's Tomb and Purana Qila. New traditions developed around these. For instance, on the day of Basant Panchmi each year, there used to be a veritable mela inside Purana Qila. Hundreds of people arrived here in festive clothes to spend the day, going home only after a communal evening meal. The mela of 1942 was the last one held in the Purana Qila, after which the circumstances of World War II and Partition, led to it being discontinued.

As it grew from a construction site into a city, New Delhi needed municipal regulation. With this in mind, Hailey, the Chief Commissioner, had created the Raisina Municipal Committee in 1916. For many years its civic responsibilities were extremely limited, as the capital site was just that, a construction site, rather than a full-fledged city. In April 1925, the Imperial Delhi Municipal Committee came into being, to deal with the growing needs of a populated city. A house tax came into effect on 1 January 1926. Over the years the Municipal Committee dealt with a range of issues, big and small.

An important part of the committee's role was the regulation of private construction within New Delhi and outlying areas such as Jangpura and Nizamuddin. Building plans were scrutinized not only to ensure that building and drainage bye-laws were not infringed, but also that 'the general idea of architectural beauty was preserved'. Control also extended to preserving order in urban spaces. To this end, in 1936-37, the committee prosecuted thirty-nine persons for failing to register their pet dogs, of which there were 1315 already registered in the city!

The Municipal Committee also concerned itself with the regulation and provision of facilities such as milk supply. Keventers Dairy started a milk delivery scheme, transporting milk around the city in large cans, each with a tap at the bottom, from which milk could be dispensed to customers. This device, however, had an unexpected drawback. The cream used to rise to the top, as a result of which most of the customers received 'weakened' milk, which they objected to. It was then proposed that milk be supplied in bottles with caps. However the outbreak of World War II prevented the bottles with their special caps being imported, so the old system continued.

Keeping the city clean was a major preoccupation of the municipal authorities, and New Delhi was often remarked on for its clean roads, in contrast not only to Old Delhi, but to other Indian cities. The capital did, however, have its problems, and malaria was one of them. There was rampant mosquito breeding in the large number of brickfields that had been created around the city, as these had pits that collected water. Defects were also found in the storm water drainage system, which were leading to stagnant water. The municipal authorities also suspected that the large number of wells in New Delhi were at fault, and a programme of filling up or hermetically sealing all of them was undertaken in 1936. Even the ornamental pools created on either side of the Central Vista, provided breeding grounds for mosquitoes. To keep the danger to a minimum, they used to be kept empty during the duration of the summer, when the Government of India migrated to Simla. Water used to be released in them in the first week of November, once the members of the higher bureaucracy returned to Delhi.

By far the most problematic factor, however, was the Kilokri sewage farm. Set up to the southeast of the city, in the area today more or less covered by Defence Colony and Lajpat Nagar, the farm was spread over some 1200 acres over which sewage from New Delhi as well Old Delhi was spread. The load of the sewage proved too much for the area and it soon became not only waterlogged but seriously polluted. Finally, in 1939, the sewage farm was closed and a modern sewage treatment plant was opened at Okhla. In the meanwhile, some of the solid waste from New Delhi was removed in lorries to the plant nursery near Safdarjung's Tomb, where it was composted by the PWD and used in the gardens. It was also used to fill the 'borrow pit' which had been created when earth had been removed to create the railway embankment.

By and large, the sanitary problems of New Delhi were easily managed. Even the Kilokri sewage farm had not been within New Delhi proper. In fact, most potentially polluting functions were kept out of New Delhi. The slaughterhouse that supplied meat to New Delhi was located in Paharganj, and when the need to build a new one was felt, it was immediately suggested that the location might be at Nizamuddin, which was close enough to the city, but not within it. New Delhi was essentially designed as a political, administrative and residential centre. No place was allocated for industrial development, which was confined to the older city and its suburbs.

New Delhi was a city of hierarchies, geared towards the convenience and amusement of the administrative elite that dominated it. It was also ordered so that each inhabitant was slotted into an appropriate place, commensurate with his race, occupation and/or rank. Nirad Chaudhuri, who arrived from Calcutta to live in Delhi in 1942, was scornful of New Delhi, a mere administrative enclave which he referred to as a ghetto, questioning whether a place with only bungalows could be called a city. One of the first things he discovered was that, 'in New Delhi streets and salaries were commensurate, and a man who unwarily gave the name of his street might find himself shunned by the denizens of certain other streets.' He went on to add, that, since however, he himself lived in Old Delhi, that put him beyond the pale altogether!

In many ways New Delhi was an unreal city, supporting and showcasing the perfect life of the colonial elite. The mundane realities of urban life—ugly industrial sites, sewage treatment plants, the poor who supplied the labour of the city, could largely be pushed outside its boundaries, to 'Old Delhi' and surrounding semi-urban areas.

The Secretariat on Independence Day, 1947

The Capital of Independent India

NEW DELHI HAD BEEN FOUNDED IN THE HOPE OF NEW beginnings. Hardinge, members of his council, George V and Crewe, saw, in the transfer of the capital, a possibility for a grand gesture, to finally convince the Indian people that the British Empire was their empire, in line with the other great empires of India's past. It was also a response to the growing demand for self-governance, as the location of the capital at Delhi was meant to free the provinces, particularly Bengal, of the thrall of a central power. Finally, it was also to bring the capital closer to the princely states, which were concentrated in north and central India, and were seen as allies and supporters of the British empire.

This vision, considered bold by its authors in 1911, was nevertheless a narrow one. Its aim was ultimately the preservation of British imperial rule, and it could, therefore, not move beyond the old traditions and hierarchies on which that rule was based. Distinctions of race and class had formed the basis on which the city had been planned; for example, in the different zones and categories of housing. The major recreational landmarks—the Gymkhana Club, the Race Course, Connaught Place—were mainly geared towards the convenience and pleasures of the elite, overwhelmingly official and white. In the decade following the inauguration, this seemed a dead city to the ordinary visitor, with large empty roads, overly neat and manicured greens, and few bustling public places.

World War II brought about changes, most obvious in the booming business in Connaught Place, but in other areas as well. A greater informality in social interactions was introduced, mainly as a result of a more mixed population. One of the consequences of the war was an increasing proportion of Indian to British officials in various rungs of the civil service. As British officers left to serve in the armed forces, their place was taken by Indian officers. Fresh recruitment of Europeans to the civil service also stopped in 1941. The official parties, therefore, now had more Indian officials, more foreign diplomats and army attachés, and journalists. The Gymkhana Club tentatively began to admit 'native elite' members in 1945.

One fallout of this sudden increase in population during the war was the need to provide more accommodation.

Housing and offices, mostly temporary structures, came up on many of the plots that had been lying vacant in New Delhi. On Queen's Way, makeshift accommodation was erected to house the large number of American soldiers who were quartered in the city. Despite this, many had to be housed in tents. The palatial houses of the maharajas were requisitioned for official purposes, and the Purana Qila became a camp for Italian prisoners of war. A new addition was the several bomb shelters that were built. The landscape was changing not only because of new structures, available space was also being used for new purposes. The golf course within the Viceregal Estate was turned over to wheat cultivation, in response to the wartime 'grow more food campaign.'

But even greater changes were on the way, as the end of the war also made the prospect of Indian independence a foreseeable reality. On the one hand this intensified the parlays of Indian political leaders with British officialdom in the corridors of power. On the other, it created a charged atmosphere in the city. Up till then, protests, riots and violence had been unknown in New Delhi. It had remained quiescent even during the Quit India movement, while Old Delhi erupted in protests, demonstrations, violence and counter-violence by government forces. Now, however, the flames were licking at its edges and tensions were simmering. A military parade to celebrate the Allied victory on 7 March 1946, faced an angry reception, with black flags being waved at it.

This was the last phase of the freedom movement, which was to culminate in Independence. The transfer of power formally took place at a midnight meeting of the Constituent Assembly in Parliament House on 14/15 August 1947. Outside, a large crowd of people in a celebratory mood had gathered, for all of Delhi had kept awake to witness this historic moment. Conch shells were blown, together with shouts of 'Mahatma Gandhi ki jai' and 'Inqilab zindabad', until all fell silent to hear Jawaharlal Nehru's voice coming over the loudspeakers, to announce to the world that 'At the stroke of the midnight hour, when the world sleeps', India had awoken 'to life and freedom'.

The next morning, Nehru was sworn in as the first Prime Minister of independent India, by the last Viceroy of British India, Lord Louis Mountbatten, within the Durbar Hall at Viceroy's House. Though the invited guests at the event were a mere five hundred or so, outside again, people had gathered in large numbers, prompting Mountbatten to remark that, 'Never have such crowds been seen within the memory of anyone I have spoken to. Not only did they line every rooftop and vantage point, but they pressed round so thick as to become finally quite unmanageable.' Through this crowd, the official party drove from Viceroy's House (which was now, once again, to be called Government House) to Parliament, for another formal ceremony.

A formal hoisting of the national flag had been planned for the evening at India Gate, to be preceded by a parade of all three divisions of the armed forces. Ultimately, the parade had to be cancelled, simply due to the huge crowds that swarmed the venue, which some officials estimated at 600,000. The ceremony was curtailed to the hoisting of the

Connaught Place on 15 August 1947

tricolour, which took place amid wild shouts of rejoicing from the assembled mass of people. As the flag unfurled, a rainbow appeared in the sky, and those witnessing it saw it as a good omen. Mountbatten remarked, 'I had never noticed how closely a rainbow could resemble the new Dominion flag of saffron, white and green.' The official festivities closed with a party at Government House, which went on till two o'clock in the morning, and which was attended by nearly 3,000, including members of the new cabinet, British and Indian army and civil officers, ambassadors, and rulers of the princely states.

Though 15 August marked a formal day when India became independent, the transfer of power was not a moment as much as a process that had been initiated some time ago. The Interim Government had been constituted in 1946, and its members had been slowly moving into the physical as well as official and social spaces within the centre of power in New Delhi. Nehru, before he moved into the Commander-in-Chief's residence nearly a year after Independence, had been living in a bungalow on 17 York Road (now Motilal Nehru Marg). Mountbatten stayed on in Government House as Governor General, until C. Rajagopalachari took over in June 1948. An important change in the function of Government House was that though originally built as a winter residence alone, it was now occupied in the summer too. The migration of the government to Simla in the summer had been curtailed by the war, and after that by the exigencies of the transfer of power. Finally, the government of independent India permanently gave up the practice. The problem from the point of view of Government House was that though the south wing, which had been designed as the First Family's living accommodation, was perfect in the winter, it was too hot in the summer, even though some rooms were air-conditioned. Though the Mountbattens moved seasonally from the south wing to the north wing, this practice was given up under the Indian incumbents, and the north wing, originally designed as a guest wing, permanently became the 'family wing'. At the end of January 1950, Dr Rajendra Prasad, who had been living at 1, Queen Victoria Road (now Rajendra Prasad Road), moved into Government House as the first President of India.

The city that had been built to house a British ruling class thus made a relatively easy transition to housing the elected representatives and bureaucracy of the independent nation. The fact that there was an overlap in personnel, particularly of the civil servants of the two regimes, made the switch easier when it came to institutions that had been created for the leisure of this elite class. The Imperial Delhi Gymkhana Club adapted quickly by simply changing its name to Delhi Gymkhana Club. It was the venue for a series of farewell parties not only for the departing British officials but for those on their way to Pakistan, including Mohammad Ali Jinnah, for whom a party with a thousand guests was held on 2 August 1947. Also in the Gymkhana Club, the 'officers of the Armed Forces of the Dominion of India', held a 'Farewell to Old Comrades Reception in honour of the Officers of the Armed Forces of the Dominion of Pakistan'.

Even as the city was celebrating the inauguration of a new era in the nation's history, storm clouds were gathering. Already there were some 70,000 refugees in Delhi, people displaced by the population transfer that had begun, between what would be the two separate nations of India and Pakistan. Even more worrying was the fact that violence had broken out in New Delhi itself. Pamela Mountbatten, the eighteen-year-old daughter of the Governor General, wrote in her diary on 7 September, 'there was a stabbing on the Estate today'. The next day there was mob violence in Connaught Place, and corner shops owned by Muslims were looted. The Prime Minister, Jawaharlal Nehru, himself arrived and tried to beat back looters with a stick in his hand. It was reported that the police and troops mostly stood by and did nothing

Mahatma Gandhi's funeral procession

but ultimately firing was ordered and some people were killed. Not even the bungalows of New Delhi were safe at this time. The Tughlaq Lane house of Badruddin Tyabji, a senior civil service officer, was looted.

The violence that had broken out in Delhi had drawn Mahatma Gandhi to the city. He arrived on 9 September and based himself at Birla House on Albuquerque Road, fasting, and holding prayer meetings there and in other parts of Delhi and in neighbouring towns.

It was here, on the evening of 30 January 1948, that he was gunned down at point-blank range by Nathuram Godse. The news of his death, which had reached most people of Delhi by radio at six o'clock in the evening, caused widespread shock. Pamela Mountbatten wrote in her diary:

'I was dumbstruck, but the announcement continued. He had been shot while he was walking to his weekly prayer meeting. By now, tears were pouring down my face.'

All cinemas, clubs and other places of entertainment were closed. Crowds of people spontaneously emerged from their homes and headed to Birla House, where the father of the nation's mortal remains had been placed on the balcony to enable many to get a last view. An even bigger crowd joined the funeral procession the next day as it left Birla House, swelling to some eight or ten lakhs by the time it reached Rajghat in the evening for the last rites.

The worst of the violence was over, but the city was subject to many strains. The violence that had been perpetrated on Muslims in both New and Old Delhi led to their being forced to seek shelter in refugee camps, set up in Purana Qila and Humayun's Tomb. These historic sites, which had once, not long before, been occupied by the villages of Indarpat and Arab ki Sarai, again returned to informal habitations. The NDMC was horrified that the manicured lawns at Humayun's Tomb would be dug up to make latrines! Some of the generous compounds of the bungalows were turned into tented refuges, including those of ministers, Nehru, Abul Kalam Azad, and Rafi Ahmad Kidwai.

While those Delhi Muslims who were fleeing violence soon left, either for Pakistan, or back to their homes, the influx of refugees from the other side of the border continued. This led to a huge population increase (between the census of 1941 and that of 1951, the population of Delhi increased by 90 per cent), which changed the face of New Delhi. It placed an immediate strain on amenities like housing and schooling, and the provision of commercial establishments.

Historic sites, once they were vacated by Muslim refugees, were used to house the newcomers, who eventually replaced tented accommodation with permanent brick structures. Soon, a school, a small dispensary, and shops transformed Humayun's Tomb into a small village, probably not very different from the settlement of Arab ki Sarai that had been removed from the monument less than forty years before. Safdarjung's Tomb was turned into a camp exclusively for women and children. Many other available open spaces of the garden city were covered with tents. The streets of New Delhi looked more crowded, and some pavements, such as in Connaught Place, began to be used by some of

The refugee camp in Humayun's Tomb

the newcomers to ply commercial trades. It was estimated that the number of squatters in the commercial areas of New Delhi increased from ninety-eight to 796 between 1947-49.

New Delhi's town planners and builders—British officialdom and also Indian contractors and entrepreneurs, had given the capital city a certain physical shape. Its British administrators, who saw it as an exclusive imperial enclave, were not destined to inhabit it long. Ultimately, the soul in the city was infused by the Indian population that would make it their own capital. The social and cultural shape it took was determined in large part by Independence and Partition.

Agrasen ki Baoli and Connaught Place

The Changing Face of New Delhi and Connaught Place

BOTH NEW DELHI AND CONNAUGHT PLACE HAVE CHANGED significantly in the more than seven decades since Independence. The years after Independence were a time for recovery from the tribulations of Partition, but also a celebration of the new nation's hopes and dreams. Nowhere were these effects felt more keenly than in Delhi. The population of Delhi as a whole grew from about 900,000 people in 1947, to 1.4 million in 1951. This dramatic increase brought challenges, but it brought new opportunities too, and nowhere more so than in Connaught Place. There was initially an ad hoc crowding of the corridors, as refugee shop owners, not finding other space, occupied verandahs and sold everything from cloth to dried fruits and stationery. This was not a long-term solution, however, and they were soon moved out to Baba Kharak Singh Marg and Panchkuian Road. Stalls were also set up along Janpath.

Not all the incoming refugees had to make do with roadside stalls. There were some who had the resources to rent space and open establishments in posh Connaught Place. Prakash Krishna arrived in Delhi from Lahore with 60,000 rupees worth of books, and set up a successful bookshop—Ramkrishna Bookshop, which survived into the 1990s. More far-flung commercial spaces were also being created. At the location where a couple of provision stores to supply the barracks of Lodi Estate during World War II had stood, a new shopping centre was built—Khan Market.

Government enterprise, too, was now entering the retail business, with a view to encouraging India's traditional crafts. These new institutions were set up in various of the temporary structures created during World War II, which had now been abandoned. The Central Cottage Industries Emporium was set up in office buildings that had been built on Janpath as offices for US army officials. Here it stayed till 1995, when it moved into the grand six-storey building it occupies today. The first set of state emporia were established in the 1960s, in a structure interestingly called the 'Theatre Communications Building'. This had literally housed the communications services of the theatre of war in the Pacific. The emporia moved to the Baba Kharak Singh buildings in the 1970s.

The restaurant business expanded after Independence, with increased demand due to the growing population. Kwality's, which had begun with ice cream, evolved into a restaurant serving Indian as well as Western cuisine. The proprietors of Kwality's built another popular restaurant, Gaylord's, with elegant Art Deco interiors. The Nirula's family was also expanding, with the Chinese Room, Delhi's first Chinese restaurant, being inaugurated in 1950. Even with the departure of the British and American clientele, there was no lack of Indians who were willing to be adventurous in the matter of cuisine. In 1960, Nirula's set up La Boheme, serving Austro-Hungarian food.

Restaurants were not only for the gay party crowd. The cafes in particular became a hub for writers, poets and artists, as was the case with Alps, and then Indian Coffee House, both on Janpath. The early post-Independence years also saw new developments in the fields of art and culture, and many of the new national cultural institutions had their beginnings in and around Connaught Place. Triveni started with one room here, and Gandharva Mahavidyalaya was housed in a building near Odeon Cinema. The Bharatiya Natya Sangh and the Bharatiya Kala Kendra were both located in Shankar Market, but later land was allotted for the latter in the Mandi House area. Mandi House in time became a cultural hub, with Triveni as well as several other institutions finding a home here.

In other areas around Connaught Place, new infrastructure, to meet the needs of the capital of a developing independent nation, was put in rapidly after Independence. A large plot of land, originally earmarked for a 'fuel plantation', was used for an exhibition ground. This was later called Pragati Maidan. The foundation stone for a Supreme Court building was laid in 1954, and that for the National Museum in 1955.

The need to house an exploding population was an early concern. New housing began to be constructed fast, though some immigrants ended up staying for years in what had initially been temporary refugee camps in places such as Purana Qila. During the course of those years, housing was also required for the growing numbers of government employees. This was because, in contrast to the limited functions of the colonial state, the government of newly independent India sought a bigger role, from making investments in industry to taking measures for the welfare of citizens.

To provide housing, large areas of land lying vacant in the eastern portion of the New Delhi site were filled in. Residential 'colonies' were built—Kaka Nagar, Bapa Nagar, Pandara Park for government officials; and Sundar Nagar and Golf Links for private owners. The vast majority of those displaced by Partition were accommodated in colonies that were spread beyond the 'core imperial area' in the blocks of land that had been far-sightedly acquired for 'future development'. These were the colonies mainly in west and south Delhi. With the rapid expansion of these new colonies, by 1953 the new administrative districts of south and west Delhi had to be created. Interestingly, these new developments in a way drew inspiration from the original garden city plan of New Delhi; so instead of compact dense plans or high-rises,

Summer fun at India Gate

they tended to favour low-rise development of bungalows on plots, with local parks and tree-lined avenues. The first few multi-storey apartments were built by the government in Rama Krishna Puram in the 1970s, but for long were the only ones of their kind.

When I first came to live in Delhi in December 1985, I lived not far from R.K. Puram, in Moti Bagh. I was, therefore, amused to read that Swinton had said in 1912 regarding the site chosen for the new capital, 'To the south the site has always been unlimited. Someday it may extend beyond Arakpur Bagmochi.' To me it seemed in 1985, and it certainly does today, more than a hundred years after Swinton's remarks, that Bagh Mochi, since renamed Moti Bagh, is very much a part of central Delhi. The urban sprawl now extends beyond even the limits of the 'enclave of Delhi' originally created in 1912, which has since become the National Capital Territory of Delhi.

Though the greater city of Delhi has grown in all directions around it, the urban area conceived of by the Town Planning Committee still has an identity of its own. It is roughly co-terminus with the area administered by the New Delhi Municipal Council, which came into being in 1994 to replace the erstwhile New Delhi Municipal Committee. Some new areas have been included within the bounds of the NDMC, mainly consisting of the diplomatic enclave on either side of Shanti Path, and some large housing colonies which, with the exception of Jor Bagh, were mainly for government employees—Lodi Colony, Chanakyapuri, Sarojini Nagar, Lakshmibai Nagar, Kidwai Nagar, Netaji Nagar and Moti Bagh.

While the area of the NDMC has been extended to some extent, the sanctity of much of the original area, with the crucial exception of Connaught Place and its surroundings, is maintained through a special designation—Lutyens' Bungalow Zone. This is inappropriately named, for neither were the bungalows designed by Lutyens, nor was the town plan exclusively his creation by any stretch of the imagination. The question of name aside, this area has retained its original character to a large extent. This can be seen in its large plots with low-rise bungalows, its wide avenues and its distinctive roundabouts. Decisions to remove some of the latter, for instance two on Janpath, south and north of its junction with Rajpath, were thankfully reversed.

Connaught Place too was changing when I arrived in Delhi in the mid-1980s. I saw the beautiful red-coloured Statesman House pulled down, to be replaced by what, in retrospect, is not a bad building at all! Jeevan Bharti, or LIC building, was even more of a shock in its sharp departure from the classical architecture of Connaught Place, though it is undoubtedly an icon of modern architecture. These and other dramatic high-rise buildings were required for a modern business district, but it could be argued that they detract from the heritage character of New Delhi's grandest shopping centre.

Ironically, as the growth of the business district was evidenced by the multiplying high-rises, the shopping centre itself declined somewhat in the 1980s and '90s. People were increasingly shopping closer home, in neighbourhood markets that were evolving into bigger centres, such as

South Extension Market and Khan Market. The restaurant business survived better, though inevitably some of the older restaurants were replaced by others. Another cause for the malaise was a deteriorating physical condition, and some years of metro construction, which inevitably disrupted infrastructure. The renaming of Connaught Place as Rajiv Chowk and Connaught Circus as Indira Chowk in 1995, seemed to underline and sum up the degradation of the heritage of this historic landmark.

Name changes, motivated by a desire to erase colonial heritage, had been taking place gradually all over Delhi. Roads were slowly renamed after Independence, with national figures replacing colonial ones. For several years there were many statues of British Viceroys and monarchs in public places, including an impressive one of George V, under a canopy designed by Lutyens, in the middle of Princes' Park. It stood there till the 1960s, when it was removed to Coronation Park, the site of the three British Imperial Durbars. For a while, controversy raged about the empty canopy—should it be removed, or should Mahatma Gandhi's statue be placed there? It survived but has remained vacant, a picturesque centerpiece to the park. The War Memorial Arch, which in any case was a monument to Indian soldiers, was easy to rededicate to nationalist rather than imperial causes, through the installation of the Amar Jawan Jyoti, the eternal flame.

There are other ways in which a capital built for an alien empire was adopted and appropriated by the people of an independent democratic nation. Republic Day celebrations began to held from 1950 on Rajpath (originally called King's Way), and in the early years, the parade passed through Connaught Place. The tricolour today flies on the dome of Rashtrapati Bhavan, (as Lutyens' Government House/Viceroy's House is now called), but interestingly, it did not appear here till the 1970s, before which it was the 'President's Standard', a special flag for the head of state, which was flown here. Flags and memorials are important markers of national identity, and what were once places for the rituals of the British Empire have been effectively reinscribed by being used for nationalist rituals. To me however, what is more significant is that the open spaces, designed for grand vistas and pageantry, are beautiful oases of green for recreation.

When they were young, my children's favourite outing was a visit to India Gate, to play in Children's Park there, to eat ice-cream or the various other snacks sold by itinerant hawkers, and buy a balloon. While they completely ignored the grand architecture of the War Memorial Arch or the princely palaces, the engine that stands in front of Baroda House, which now houses offices of the Northern Railways, always merited a joyful examination. India Gate has become one of the largest recreational spaces in Delhi, and since the entertainments it offers cost relatively little or nothing, it is an inclusive place.

Much of New Delhi is occupied by institutional buildings, and there are particular clusters of these. There is of course the area around Mandi House, which is a hub of various cultural institutions and venues. Lodi Estate, the area often known by planners and architects as Steinabad after the architect Joseph

The Habitat Centre

Stein, who designed many of the buildings there, offers a mix of office, institutional and cultural buildings adjoining one of Delhi's best parks, Lodi Garden. Notable among these are the India International Centre and the Habitat Centre, both of which offer cultural activities that include theatre, films, music, talks and seminars and are the city's most popular venues for book launches, as well as a variety of cuisine in their restaurants. Another iconic cultural hub, that is in the process of profound change, is Pragati Maidan. The decision to redevelop it as a convention centre led to the demolition, in 2017, of several structures within this exhibition ground. Not only did the city lose iconic buildings, the most prominent being the Hall of Nations, it lost the memories of a generation that had watched movies at Shakuntalam Theatre, and have over the years attended the annual Trade Fair, or the Book Fairs at Pragati Maidan.

New Delhi, or Lutyens' Delhi as people often call it, cannot completely shake off its aura of power and influence. It is, after all, where many of the richest and most powerful of the country live, in large bungalows, as others did when the city was first built. From time to time this very character is questioned—why is so much space being 'wasted'? Would it not be a more economical use of land to replace the bungalows with denser built-up areas, even maybe high-rises?

The bungalows of New Delhi do house a political and social elite, but the neighbourhood they live in is still much more inclusive than, say, gated apartment complexes. There are wide pavements that anyone might walk on, enjoying the shade of the large avenue trees. Though the boundary walls have risen higher in this age where 'security' is an important concern, one can still admire some of the bungalow architecture, such as that of Mohammad Ali Jinnah's erstwhile house on 10 Abdul Kalam Marg (until 2017, Aurangzeb Road). Some houses such as Teen Murti House, which was originally the Commander-in-Chief's residence and then that of the first Prime Minister, Jawaharlal Nehru, is now open to the public as a museum.

There are upmarket shopping areas, such as Khan Market, but they are more inclusive than shut-off air-conditioned malls. In Khan Market you will find fashion designers cheek by jowl with old-fashioned 'general stores' as well as itinerant fruit-sellers. There are also small neighbourhood markets, such as that on Krishna Menon Lane, off Krishna Menon Marg (originally Hastings Road). When I first met my husband, many years before we got married, he used to patronize a barber in that market, which was right next to his home on 8 Krishna Menon Marg. This sprawling bungalow, one of a series that were built on this road for Secretaries to Government, had an intriguing sandstone fountain in the back garden. Like many others, my husband's family were transient occupants and moved out a few years later. Only many years afterwards did I find out, through a photograph of the house preserved in the collection of the Royal Institute of British Architects, that Herbert Baker had lived in this bungalow when it was newly built!

Each of the large bungalows still contains its numerous 'servants' quarters'. In an age when the numbers of domestic staff have shrunk to levels much below what the British officials were accustomed to, they are occupied by a somewhat more diverse population, which often has a life independent of the life of the bungalow. Long after my husband's family moved

Connaught Place today

Connaught Place at night

out of Krishna Menon Marg, the dhobi who lived in one of those quarters, continued to do so, and ran a service that took in laundry from a wide network, including our family. The back lanes, on to which these quarters open, have a character of their own, not always visible to those who drive down the main avenues. The market on Krishna Menon Lane is very much a part of that world.

Connaught Place too has evolved, though it is still popularly called that. The official name, Rajiv Chowk, did not take, except perhaps in the context of the Metro station located there. The Metro has connected it to far-flung areas in the National Capital Region, and a variety of visitors pour in, shoppers and restaurant-goers from Delhi's colonies, Civil Lines, or Old Delhi, as well as students from the North Campus of Delhi university. A partial makeover and restoration was initiated in preparation for the Commonwealth Games in

2010, and it has corrected some of the problems with the aging structures.

Though many of the older retail outlets have closed, many new ones have opened in their place—such as high street brands for whom 'Connaught Place' is a desirable address to have in their list of outlets. Some of the old restaurants, such as Gaylords and Volga, have closed down, but there are some old survivors like Wenger's, Kwality's, or United Coffee House, which has been revamped. There is a plethora of restaurants, bars and coffee shops that flourish, and new places like Junkyard Café, Bombay Brasserie, Tamasha and Lord of the Drinks, are very popular with the young crowd. The closing of the venerable Regal, which shut its doors in 2017, is a sad loss for the nostalgic, but new screens and multiplexes have been replacing the old, rather worn infrastructure, leading to a revival, and attracting a new crowd. Both the old Plaza and Rivoli cinemas have been bought over by PVR Cinemas, and are now stylish multiplexes. The Odeon Cinema, once a regular halt for filmgoers, on the other hand, has metamorphosed into a bar and multicuisine restaurant, named Odeon Social.

Connaught Place has managed to reinvent itself, to keep pace with the times, and give the new swanky malls that have opened up around the city, a run for their money. Connaught Place offers some distinct things few malls have. Apart from the shopping, eating and movie watching, it is a public space, though its details have changed over the years. The very British bandstand was removed after Independence, to be replaced in 1970 with a system of fountains which ran for a while. Today the grassy green expanses in the middle are a refreshing oasis for visitors; a hangout for the young on most days, and for families on weekends. The corridors and pavements fronting the buildings are the place to browse among hawkers' wares and eat street food. It is a happy, more inclusive, reinvention of a space where once only those shopping at the establishments proclaiming themselves 'by appointment to the Viceroy' trod. A long-standing tradition has been to ring in the New Year with a joyous party in Connaught Place, though fears that these revels will turn raucous often leads to police precautions and restrictions.

Connaught Place, or for that matter New Delhi as a whole, have come a long way from the days of the British Raj. Contrary to what one might imagine, they are not places for those essentially seeking nostalgia. They have been reimagined to serve the needs of a democratic state and for an Indian people. That is what gives them continued relevance in the twenty-first century, and for new generations.

There is much to celebrate in New Delhi, even if one is not lucky enough to live there. The significant number of large trees provide a crucial green lung in the middle of a city that is suffering from dangerous levels of air pollution. Its institutional, commercial and public spaces are immensely popular among visitors from all parts of the city. For those who are sensitive to heritage, New Delhi represents the last in the series of capital cities built in Delhi. It stands for an important era in the world's history. This was when the British Empire felt the need to reinvent itself, and to do so, it drew upon the traditions of the great Indian empires, such as the Mughal. Not only does the main avenue of New Delhi align Government House with Purana Qila, it lies parallel to the main ceremonial avenue of Shahjahanabad, the street we today call Chandni Chowk. The town plan of New Delhi also has certain unique features, such as the system of radial roads leading out from roundabouts.

Conservationists have long been arguing for a greater need to recognize and protect New Delhi. One of the outcomes was the decision to include New Delhi along with Shahjahanabad in an application to UNESCO, for recognizing both under the category of World Heritage City, under the title 'Delhi's Imperial Capital Cities'. The application was withdrawn by the government in 2015, and hence the nomination did not proceed.

Whether or not the city gets UNESCO recognition in

A typical New Delhi avenue

the future, there is no doubt that it needs to be preserved in its essentials, particularly its characteristic town plan. Densification beyond a certain point would put more traffic on the roads than the roundabouts can handle, and necessitate the cutting down of the trees that provide valuable green cover. It would change the essential features of the town plan. The world as well as India would lose one of its most beautiful and distinctive historic cities.

Notes

1. *The Historical Record of the Imperial Visit to India: 1911*, John Murray, London, 1914, pp 174-5.
2. Robert Grant Irving, *Indian Summer: Lutyens, Baker and Imperial Delhi*, Yale University Press, New Haven 1981, p 13; Lord Hardinge of Penhurst, *My Indian Years 1910-1916*, John Murray, London, 1948, pp 55-6.
3. Quoted in David Johnson, *New Delhi: The Last Imperial City*, Kindle edition, p 40.
4. Johnson, *New Delhi*, pp 60-1, 63.
5. Johnson, *New Delhi*, p 51; Malvika Singh, Rudrangshu Mukherjee and Pramod Kapoor, *New Delhi: Making of a Capital*, Roli Books, New Delhi, 2009, p 20.
6. Sir John Thompson, 'Delhi as Capital, Proceedings of the East India Association', 7.2.1933, *Asiatic Review*, v 29, 1933, p 229.
7. Johnson, *New Delhi*, p 53.
8. Irving, *Indian Summer*, p 34.
9. Johnson, *New Delhi*, pp 55, 58.
10. Johnson, *New Delhi*, pp 41-2, 64, 107.
11. Irving, *Indian Summer*, p 27.
12. Irving, *Indian Summer*, p 18.
13. Hardinge to Crewe, 25 August 1911, in John Capper, Delhi, the Capital of India, Asian Educational Services, New Delhi, 1997 (reprint of 1918 edition), Appendix, p xlvi.
14. Johnson, *New Delhi*, pp 37-8.
15. Swapna Liddle, *Chandni Chowk: The Mughal City of Old Delhi*, Speaking Tiger, Delhi, 2017, p 5.
16. Irving, *Indian Summer*, p 12.

17. Irving, *Indian Summer*, pp 29-34; Johnson, New Delhi, pp 68-9.
18. Irving, *Indian Summer*, pp 23-4, 33; Johnson, New Delhi, pp 66, 69, 72 80-1.
19. *Laying-out, &c, of the New Capital of India, Delhi*, vol I, p 4b.
20. Ibid., pp13, 25-39, 46-7.
21. Ibid., pp 32, 61, 78; The artist Reginald Barrat, to Sir Valentine Chirol, dated 9 February, 1912, ibid., p 82.
22. Ibid., pp 61, 105, 102, 107; Secretary of State to Hardinge, 12 March and 21 March 1912, Ibid., pp 112, 126.
23. Note by Louis Dane, Lt. Govr. of Punjab, dated 11 January 1912, Ibid., pp 69-70, 119.
24. 'Report of the Delhi Town Planning Committee on its choice of site for the new imperial capital at Delhi, 13 July 1912', in Mushirul Hasan and Dinyar Patel, eds. *From Ghalib's Dilli to New Delhi: A Documentary Record*, pp 130-41.
25. David A. Johnson, 'Competing Visions of Empire in the Colonial Built Environment: Sir Bradford Leslie and the Building of New Delhi', *Britain and the World,* 8.1 (2015): pp 47-9.
26. 'Report of the Delhi Town Planning Committee', pp 134-40.
27. *Laying-out, &c, of the New Capital of India, Delhi*, vol 2, p 239; Johnson, 'Competing Visions of Empire', pp 41-3, 48-9.
28. Lutyens to Emily, 18 June 1912, Clayre Percy and Jane Ridley eds, *The Letters of Edwin Lutyens to His Wife Lady Emily*, Hamish Hamilton, London, 1985, p 254.
29. *Laying-out, &c, of the New Capital of India, Delhi*, vol, p 176, particularly, first report of H.V. Lanchester, pp 180-4.
30. For this and the following, see notes by Hardinge, 16 July 1912 and 31 July 1912, and Hardinge to Reginald Craddock dated 30 July 1912, Craddock to Hardinge 31 July 1912. Ibid., pp 198-201, 235-9, 241.

31. Note by Hardinge, dated 14 August 1912, and letter to Swinton, dated 6 October 1912, *Laying-out, &c, of the New Capital of India, Delhi*, vol 2, pp 9-11; 100.
32. Hardinge to Lutyens, dated 17 September 1912; Swinton to Hardinge, dated 20 September 1912, Ibid., pp 77 and 85.
33. Irving, *Indian Summer*, pp 56, 62-4; Hardinge to Swinton, dated 8 September 1912; reply dated 3 October; Lutyens to Hardinge, dated 11 October 1912, Hardinge to Lutyens, dated 6 November 1912; *Laying-out, &c, of the New Capital of India, Delhi*, vol 2, pp 9-10, 46, 77, 95-6, 107, 120.
34. Town Planning Committee's Report on the south site, *Laying-out, &c, of the New Capital of India, Delhi*, vol 2, pp 240-9, 257.
35. Ibid., pp 144, 248, 261-2.
36. Irving, *Indian Summer*, pp 67-70.
37. *Laying-out, &c, of the New Capital of India*, Delhi, vol 2, pp 89-90.
38. Irving, *Indian Summer*, pp 46-7, 92-8; Johnson, New Delhi, p 120.
39. *The Historical Record of the Imperial Visit to India*, p 211; *Laying-out, &c, of the New Capital of India, Delhi*, vol 1, pp 202-3; *Laying-out, &c, of the new Capital of India, Delhi*, vol 2, pp 1-2, 5, 48-70, 74-6, 80-3.
40. Irving, *Indian Summer*, pp 103-4; Letter from Hardinge to Valentine Chirol dated 12 February 1912, in *Laying-out, &c, of the New Capital of India, Delhi*, vol 1, p 105.
41. Thomas R. Metcalf, *An Imperial Vision: Indian Architecture and Britain's Raj*, Oxford University Press, New Delhi, 2002, pp 212-13
42. *Laying-out, &c, of the new Capital of India, Delhi*, vol 2, pp 1-3, 25-7, 366a, 242; Metcalf, *An Imperial Vision*, p 219; Irving, *Indian Summer*, pp 101-02.

43. Singh, Mukherjee and Kapoor, *New Delhi*, pp 38-9; Swinton to Hardinge, 3rd October 1912, *Laying-out, &c, of the New Capital of India, Delhi*, vol 2, p 96.
44. Swinton to Hardinge, 10 October 1912, Lutyens to Hardinge 1 November 1912, *Laying-out, &c, of the New Capital of India, Delhi*, vol 2, pp 106-7, 118.
45. Memorandum by Hardinge, 13 January 1913, Ibid., pp 154-5.
46. Memorandum by Hardinge, 13 January 1913, Ibid., p 155; Metcalf, *An Imperial Vision*, pp 225, 229; Irving, *Indian Summer*, pp 97-8.
47. Irving, *Indian Summer*, p 115; Johnson, New Delhi, pp 114, 117-18; *Laying-out, &c, of the New Capital of India, Delhi*, vol 2, pp 38-41, 79, 93, 176a-76b, 199-200, 231-3.
48. Johnson, *New Delhi*, pp 161, 170. This and the following from 'Report on the acquisition of land for the imperial capital at Delhi', in Hasan and Patel, eds, *From Ghalib's Dilli to New Delhi*, pp 160-74.
49. *Laying-out, &c, of the New Capital of India, Delhi*, vol 2, pp 132-4, 146-51.
50. *Laying-out, &c, of the New Capital of India, Delhi*, vol 3, pp 109, 151, 167; Narayani Gupta, 'Delhi's history as reflected in its toponymy', in Mala Dayal, ed., *Celebrating Delhi*, Ravi Dayal Publisher, New Delhi, 2010, p 98; Layout plan of Jangpura in Pilar Maria Gueirrieri, *Negotiating Cultures: Delhi's Architecture and Planning 1912-1962*, Oxford University Press, New Delhi, 2018, p 82.
51. Johnson, *New Delhi*, pp 172-8; J. Addison, 'Report on the land acquisition proceedings at Delhi', p 53; 'Third and Sixty-sixth meetings of the IDC, 11 April and 8 January 1915 respectively, *Laying-out, &c, of the New Capital of India, Delhi*, vol 2, pp 363, 376.

52. Baker, speech at the Proceedings of the East India Association, 7.2.1933; Asiatic Review, v 29, 1933, p 236.
53. *Laying-out, &c, of the New Capital of India, Delhi*, vol 2, p 112.
54. Note on 'The question of the treatment of mosques, temples, and tombs in connection with land acquisition proceedings at Delhi', in Hasan and Patel, *Ghalib's Dilli to Lutyens' New Delhi*, pp 197- 221.
55. Maulvi Zafar Hasan, *List of Hindu and Mohammedan Monuments of Delhi Province*, volume II, Delhi, 1919.
56. *The Letters of Edwin Lutyens*, p 382.
57. *Laying-out, &c, of the New Capital of India, Delhi*, vol 3, pp 105, 401; Proceedings of the Imperial Delhi Committee for the Month of December 1915, Home Department Public Proceedings, National Archives of India.
58. *Laying-out, &c, of the New Capital of India, Delh*i, vol 3, p 194.
59. Proceedings of ninth meeting of the Imperial Delhi Committee, held on 23 May 1913, Home Department Public Proceedings.
60. Proceedings of the first meeting of the Imperial Delhi Committee, held on 27 March 1913, *Laying-out, &c, of the New Capital of India, Delhi*, vol 2, 359.
61. Alexander Rouse, speech at the Proceedings of the East India Association, 7.2.1933; *Asiatic Review*, v 29, 1933, p 240.
62. Irving, *Indian Summer*, p 142.
63. Swinton to Hardinge 10 October 1912, *Laying-out, &c, of the New Capital of India, Delhi*, vol 2, p 106.
64. Baker to Hardinge 6 August 1913, *Laying-out, &c, of the New Capital of India, Delhi*, vol 3, pp 70-1.
65. Correspondence between Hardinge, Lutyens and Baker, *Laying-out, &c, of the New Capital of India, Delhi*, vol 2, pp -335-39, 349-50.

66. Metcalf, *An imperial vision*, pp 223-24; Johnson, New Delhi, pp 123-4.
67. Irving, *Indian Summer*, p 42; Lutyens to Hardinge, 30 May 1913, *Laying-out, &c, of the New Capital of India, Delhi*, vol 2, pp 409-10; Swinton to Hardinge, 7 August 1913, *Laying-out, &c, of the New Capital of India, Delhi*, vol 3, pp 71-2. Hardinge to Hailey, 13 August 1913, Ibid., p 75.
68. Swinton to Hardinge, 7 August 1913, Hailey to Hardinge, 16 August 1913; Hailey to DuBoulay, 3 September 1913, Ibid., pp 72-72a; 76-7; 96-7.
69. Joseph King, *Empire and Craftsmanship*, privately printed, Plymouth, 1913; Ibid., pp 277, 288, 304-05.
70. Ibid., pp 253, 261.
71. Johnson, *New Delhi*, p 133.
72. 72. *Laying-out, &c, of the New Capital of India, Delhi*, vol 2, p 243.
73. *Laying-out, &c, of the New Capital of India, Delhi*, vol 1, pp 88h, 69-70
74. King, *Colonial Urban Development*, pp 255-6.
75. Ibid., p 259.
76. *New Capital at Delhi, Preliminary Report and Estimate*, Simla, Government Central Branch Press, 1912. 'Estimate no. IV—Domestic Water Supply; Report dated 12 September 1912 by Mr H.E. Parker, assistant sanitary engineer, on the probable cost of domestic water supply, p 30.
77. Letter from the Military Secretary to the Viceroy, to the Secretary, Imperial Delhi Committee, 19 September 1914, in Home Department Public Proceedings, March, 1915, no. 38, in the National Archives of India.
78. *New Capital at Delhi, Preliminary Report and Estimate*, 'General Report dated 1 October 1912 by Mr T.R.J. Ward, C.I.E.,

M.V.O., superintending engineer, on the preliminary reports and estimates for building the new Capital at Delhi', pp 21-3.

79. King, *Colonial Urban Development*, p 268; 'Estimate no. IV—Domestic Water Supply', p 30; Johnson, *New Delhi*, pp 152-3; *Laying-out, &c, of the New Capital of India, Delhi*, vol 2, pp 214-23.

80. Johnson, *New Delhi*, pp, 154-5.

81. Chandra Narayan Mathur to Hardinge, undated. *Laying-out, &c, of the New Capital of India, Delhi*, vol 3, pp 427-30.

82. Hardinge to George Birdwood, 18 August 1913, Ibid., pp 78-9; 'Estimate no. IV—Domestic Water Supply', p 29.

83. Hardinge, note of 31 July 1912, in *Laying-out, &c, of the New Capital of India, Delhi*, vol 1, p 237

84. Johnson, *New Delhi*, p 158.

85. King, *Colonial Urban Development*, pp 266-7.

86. J.S. Hardman to A.V. Askwith, 9 February 1942. Chief Commissioner's Records, Delhi State Archives.

87. Speech by Lutyens at the Proceedings of the East India Association, 7.2.1933; *Asiatic Review*, v 29, 1933 pp 233.

88. *Laying-out, &c, of the new Capital of India, Delhi*, vol 3, pp 56, 60b-62.

89. Andreas Volwahsen, *Imperial Delhi*, Timeless Books, Delhi, 2002, pp 216-17.

90. *Laying-out, &c, of the New Capital of India, Delhi*, vol 2, pp 245-46.

91. Notes by T.R.J. Ward and P.H. Clutterbuck, Conservator of Forests, Ibid., pp 22-5, 27-9.

92. Enclosure in letter of Hailey to DuBoulay, 20 April 1914, *Laying- out, &c, of the New Capital of India, Delhi*, vol 3, p 251. The saying is originally attributed to the fourteenth century

Sufi saint Nizamuddin Auliya. Its meaning is similar to 'there's many a slip between the cup and the lip.'
93. Ibid., pp 28-9.
94. Letter of R.P. Russell, Secretary to GOI, Public Works, 21 March 1914, and Hardinge to Holderness, 16 June 1914, Ibid., pp 21-3, 33, 138-9, 224-7, 295.
95. Letter from Lutyens and Baker to Secretary, Imperial Delhi Committee, 17 March 1914, Ibid., pp 167, 247, 233.
96. Ibid., pp 260, 345-51, 395.
97. Ibid., pp 333, 375-6, 470-1.
98. Correspondence between Hardinge and Hailey, dated 20 and 30 November, 1 and 2 December 1914, Ibid., pp 340-3.
99. Chelmsford to Hardinge, 18 August 1916, quoted in Johnson, *New Delhi*, p 119.
100. Hailey to DuBoulay, 7 January 1915, reply dated 9 January, *Laying-out, &c, of the New Capital of India, Delhi*, vol 3, pp 360-1; and p 418
101. Progress report for the month ending 30 September 1915, *Proceedings of the Imperial Delhi Committee for the Month of December 1915*, Part A, no. 8.
102. Proceedings of the one hundred and first meeting of the IDC, 18 February 1916, *Layingout, &c, of the New Capital of India, Delhi*, vol 3, pp 476-9.
103. Lutyens to Hardinge, 4 March 1916, Ibid., pp 480-1; Progress report for the month ending 30 September 1915, *Proceedings of the Imperial Delhi Committee for the Month of December 1915*, Part A, no. 8.
104. Hardinge to Hailey, 13 March 1916, *Laying-out, &c, of the New Capital of India, Delhi*, vol 3, pp 484-7.
105. Hardinge, *My Indian Years*, pp 121-2; Hardinge to Hailey, 18

March 1916, *Laying-out, &c, of the New Capital of India, Delhi,* vol 3, pp 491-2.
106. *Laying-out, &c, of the New Capital of India, Delhi,* vol 2, pp 4d-5, 202, 207-08, 230-230b, 377, 489; *Proceedings of the Imperial Delhi Committee for the Month of December 1915,* Part A, no. 8.
107. The forty-seventh meeting of the IDC, 11 and 12 June, 1914, Ibid., p 299; Annual Progress Report for New Capital Project at Delhi, 1924-25; Chief Commissioner's Records, Financial, 49/1929, Part B; *The Letters of Edwin Lutyens,* pp 341-2, 376.
108. DuBoulay to F.A. Maxwell, Military Secretary to the Viceroy, 22 February 1915, Maxwell to Hailey, 22/23 February 1915; Lutyens to DuBoulay, 1 March 1916, *Laying-out, &c, of the New Capital of India, Delhi,* vol 3, pp 370, 378-9, 383.
109. Hardinge to Holderness, 10 June 1914, *Laying-out, &c, of the New Capital of India, Delhi,* vol 3, p 293; Progress report for the month ending 30 September 1915, *Proceedings of the Imperial Delhi Committee for the Month of December 1915,* Part A, no. 8; Annual Progress Report for New Capital Project at Delhi, 1921-22.
110. Irving, *Indian Summer,* pp 126, 139.
111. Annual Progress Report for New Capital Project at Delhi, 1923-24, 1924-25, 1926-27, 1930-31.
112. Ibid. 1923-24, 1925-26, 1927-28, 1929-30, 1931-32.
113. Johnson, *New Delhi,* pp 148-9; Annual Progress Report for New Capital Project at Delhi, 1925-26.
114. Johnson, *New Delhi,* pp 149-50.
115. Johnson, *New Delhi,* pp 150-2.
116. Annual Progress Report for New Capital Project at Delhi, 1926-27.
117. Annual Progress Report for New Capital Project at Delhi, 1921-22, 1922-23.

118. Annual Progress Report for New Capital Project at Delhi, 1927- 28, 1929-30; Irving, *Indian Summer*, p 140; *The Letters of Edwin Lutyens*, p 417.
119. Annual Progress Report for New Capital Project at Delhi, 1921-22.
120. Annual Progress Report for New Capital Project at Delhi, 1924-25, 1927-28.
121. Irving, *Indian Summer*, pp 124-5.
122. Singh, Mukherjee and Kapoor, New Delhi, p 226; Hindustan Times quoted in Stephen Legg, *Spaces of Colonialism: Delhi's Urban Governmentalities*, Blackwell Publishing, 2007, p 35
123. *The Illustrated Weekly of India*, 1 March, 1931.
124. Singh, Mukherjee and Kapoor, *New Delhi*, p 227.
125. Irving, Indian Summer, pp 139-40; *Laying-out, &c, of the new Capital of India, Delhi*, vol 2, pp 208a-208b; 347-8.
126. Lutyens, speech at the Proceedings of the East India Association, 7.2.1933; *Asiatic Review*, v 29, 1933, p 234.
127. Irving, *Indian Summer*, p 130.
128. Annual Progress Report for New Capital Project at Delhi, 1921-22.
129. Hardinge to Lutyens, 17 June, 4 August, 1913, Lutyens to Hardinge 12 September 1913, *Laying-out, &c, of the New Capital of India, Delhi*, vol 3, pp 18, 68a-68b, 99-100.
130. Chief Engineer Delhi, to Secretary IDC, 10 November 1915, *Proceedings of the Imperial Delhi Committee for the Month of December 1915*, Part A, no.1.
131. Irving, *Indian Summer*, p 174.
132. Annual Progress Report for New Capital Project at Delhi, 1925-26.
133. Andreas Volwahsen, *Imperial Delhi*, pp 187-8.
134. *Laying-out, &c, of the New Capital of India, Delhi*, vol 2, pp 393-4.

135. Correspondence between Madho Singh and DuBoulay, 5 and 10 March 1915, and DuBoulay and R.P. Russell (PWD), 11 and 16 March 1915, *Laying-out, &c, of the new Capital of India, Delhi*, vol 3, pp 385-6, 388, 393.
136. Correspondence between Lutyens and Hardinge, 30 June, 28 July, 2 September, 1915, Ibid., pp 407-08, 414-15, 426, 430-1.
137. *Laying-out, &c, of the New Capital of India, Delhi*, vol 2, pp 153-4; vol 1, pp 4c-4d, 58, 146, 149, 157, 122-3.
138. *Laying-out, &c, of the New Capital of India, Delhi*, vol 3, pp 364-8.
139. Hardinge to Hailey, 7 February 1916, Ibid., p 469.
140. Irving, *Indian Summer*, p 141.
141. Annual Progress Report for the New Capital Project at Delhi, 1925-26, 1927-28.
142. Lutyens to Hardinge, 30 July 1915, *Laying-out, &c, of the New Capital of India, Delhi*, vol 3, pp 415-16
143. Percy Brown to Viceroy, 8 November 1930.
144. Correspondence between Constance Villiers-Stuart and Hardinge, 29 October 1913, 1 December 1913, 22 January 1914, 7 May 1914, 24 May 1914, *Laying-out, &c, of the New Capital of India, Delhi*, vol 3, pp 120a-20b, 131, 160, 261-2, 277; *The letters of Edwin Lutyens*, p 342.
145. Rajendar Lal, *Dilli mein das varsh*, p 35.
146. Deputy Secy PWD, to President IDC, 27 November 1915, *Proceedings of the Imperial Delhi Committee for the Month of December 1915*, Part A, no. 5.
147. Partha Mitter, 'The Politics of Architectural Decoration', in Partha Mitter and Naman P. Ahuja, eds. *The Arts and Architecture of Rashtrapati Bhavan: Lutyens and Beyond*, Publications Division, Government of India, New Delhi, 2016, pp 124-57.

148. Robert Byron, *New Delhi*, p 8; Annual Progress Report for the New Capital Project at Delhi, 1928-29.
149. Annual Progress Report for New Capital Project at Delhi, 1927-28, 1930-31; Sumanta K. Bhowmick, *Princely Palaces in New Delhi*, Niyogi Books, New Delhi, 2016, passim; Annual Progress Report for New Capital Project at Delhi, 1927-28.
150. Maurice Dekobra, *Perfumed Tigers: Adventures in the Land of the Maharajahs*, Cassell & Company Ltd., London, 1931, pp 204-5.
151. J.S. Middleton of Messers Ranken & Co. to Hardinge, 23 December 1911 and reply dated 25 December, *Laying-out, &c, of the New Capital of India, Delhi*, vol 1, pp 19-21.
152. Town Planning Committee's Report on the south site, ibid., vol 2, p 247.
153. *Letters of Edwin Lutyens*, p 292; Irving, *Indian Summer*, pp 311, 314.
154. R.C. Arora, *Delhi, the Imperial City*, Unique Literature Publishing House, Aligarh, 1953, p 79; Gopal Krishn, *Delhi in Two Days*, p 68.
155. Pran Nevile, *Carefree Days: Many Roles, Many Lives*, Kindle Edition, loc 508, 538; Kartar Lalvani,*The Making of India: The Untold Story of British Enterprise*, Bloomsbury, London, New York, 2016.
156. Annual Progress Report for New Capital Project at Delhi, 1925-26, 1926-27, 1927-28, 1929-30.
157. Gopal Krishn, *Delhi in Two Days*, p 68; Ranjana Sengupta, *Delhi Metropolitan: The Making of an Unlikely City*, Penguin Books, New Delhi 2007, p 217.
158. Annual Progress Report for New Capital Project at Delhi, 1929-30, 1931-32; *Delhi 4 Shows: Talkies of Yesteryear*, Kindle edition, loc 332-42; Sengupta, *Delhi Metropolitan*, p 217.

159. Avishek G. Dastidar, 'The heart of Delhi, even then', *Hindustan Times*, 1 September 2011; *Delhi 4 Shows*, loc 394, 487; New Delhi Municipality, Annual Report for 1939-40; *The New Delhi Directory, 1929-30*.
160. Annual Progress Report for New Capital Project at Delhi, 1925-26, 1926-27, 1927-28, 1929-30, 1931-32; Chaudhuri, *Autobiography*, loc. 12778; New Delhi Municipality, Annual Report for 1939-40.
161. Andreas Augustin, *The Imperial, New Delhi*, The Most Famous Hotels in the World, n.d., pp 48-53.
162. Gopal Krishn, *Delhi in Two Days*, p 68.
163. *The New Delhi Directory, 1929-30*; Nevile, *Carefree Days*, loc 491; Manoj Sharma, 'A number of shops in Connaught Place boast of a rich legacy', *Hindustan Times*, 1 September 2011.
164. *The New Delhi Directory*, 1929-30; Sengupta, *Delhi Metropolitan*, p 219; Tristram Hunt, *Ten Cities that Made an Empire*, p 306.
165. *The New Delhi Directory*, 1929-30; Preetika Rana, 'Wenger's: New Delhi's Oldest Bakery', *Wall Street Journal*, 21 December 2011.
166. *The New Delhi Directory*, 1929-30; Mayank Austen Sufi, 'The book lover's Connaught Place', *Hindustan Times*, 15 January 2011; Manoj Sharma, 'A number of shops in Connaught Place boast of a rich legacy', *Hindustan Times*, 1 September 2011; Mayank Austen Sufi, 'India's oldest toy story', *Live Mint*, 11 March 2011.
167. *The New Delhi Directory*, 1929-30.
168. Pothen, *Glittering Decades*, loc. 1159-84, 1280-90, 1424, 1967; Lal, *Dilli mein das varsh*, pp 49-53.
169. Lalit Nirula, 'Growing up in CP', from 'Dilli Meri Jaan—a symposium', *Seminar*, December 2011.

170. Sourish Bhattacharya, 'Know the story behind Kwality, Delhi's favourite spot to munch on chana-bhatura', *India Today*, 11 September, 2016.
171. Chief Engineer's note dated 23.4.1929, Chief Commissioner's Records, Financial, 49/1929, Part B.
172. Chief Engineer's note dated 23.4.1929, Chief Commissioner's Records, Financial, 49/1929, Part B; Annual Progress Report for New Capital Project at Delhi, 1931-32.
173. Chaudhuri, *Autobiography*, loc. 12564.
174. Note by George Swinton, 12 December 1912, *Laying-out, &c, of the New Capital of India, Delhi*, vol 2, p 144.
175. Memorandum by Sir T. Wyne, Ibid., p 91.
176. Legg, *Spaces of Colonialism*, p 91.
177. Proposals for the layout of the educational buildings in New Delhi, *Proceedings of the Imperial Delhi Committee*, Part A, nos. 73-77; *Report of the Indian Retrenchment Committee, 1922-23*, p 196.
178. Aparna Basu, 'The Foundation of Delhi University', in R.E Frykenberg ed. *Delhi Through the Ages*, Oxford University Press, New Delhi, 1986.
179. Proposals for the layout of the educational buildings in New Delhi, *Proceedings of the Imperial Delhi Committee*, Part A, nos. 73-77.
180. Ajay Kumar Sharma, *A History of Educational Institutions in Delhi 1911-1961*, Sanbun Publishers, New Delhi, 2011; Annual Progress Report for New Capital Project at Delhi, 1929- 30, 1931-32; I am grateful to Rana Sen for information on Raisina Bengali School.
181. King, *Colonial Urban Development*, p 27; Annual Progress Report for New Capital Project at Delhi, 1926-27, 1927-28.
182. Annual Progress Report for New Capital Project at Delhi, 1926-27
183. Irving, *Indian Summer*, p 331.

184. King, *Colonial Urban Development*, p 273.
185. Annual Progress Report for New Capital Project at Delhi, 1926-27, 1930-31.
186. DuBoulay to H. Wheeler, Home Secretary, dated 11 February 1913, *Laying-out, &c, of the New Capital of India, Delhi*, vol 2, pp 199-200.
187. Chaudhuri, *Autobiography of an Unknown Indian*, loc. 12826.
188. Annual Progress Report for New Capital Project at Delhi, 1921-22, 1923-24, 1927-28, 1928-29; New Delhi Municipality, Annual Report for 1938-39, 1939-40
189. *Census of India*, 1931, Manager of Publications, Delhi, 1933, p 19; *Census of India*, 1971, Controller of Publications, 1975, p 59.
190. *Laying-out, &c, of the New Capital of India, Delhi*, vol 1, p 53
191. *Laying-out, &c, of the New Capital of India, Delhi*, vol 3, pp 47-56; Johnson, *New Delhi*, p 155; King, *Colonial Urban Development*, p 272; Annual Progress Report for New Capital Project at Delhi, 1927-28, 1928-29.
192. Chaudhuri, *Autobiography*, loc. 12944, 12935.
193. Annual Progress Report for New Capital Project at Delhi, 1926-27.
194. Dekobra, *Perfumed Tigers*, pp 206-07.
195. Chief Commissioner's Records, File no. 3(29) 1942 L.S.G.; New Delhi Municipality, Annual Report for 1936-37.
196. Lal, *Dilli mein das varsh*, pp 111-12.
197. New Delhi Municipality, Annual Report for 1936-37.
198. New Delhi Municipality, Annual Report for 1938-39, and 1939. (Health Department), p 15.
199. New Delhi Municipality, Annual Report for 1936-37, 1938-39.
200. New Delhi Municipality, Annual Report for 1939 (Health Department), p 16.
201. New Delhi Municipality, Annual Report for 1936-37, 1938-39.

202. New Delhi Municipality, Annual Report for 1936-37; 1937-38.
203. King, *Colonial Urban Development*, p 258; New Delhi Municipality, Annual Report for 1936-37.
204. Chaudhuri, *Autobiography*, Kindle edition, loc. 12207, 12537-12554.
205. Pothen, *Glittering Decades*, passim.
206. Chaudhuri, *Autobiography*, loc. 12797; Pothen, *Glittering Decades*, loc.1220-1268; Rajendar Lal, *Dilli mein das varsh*, pp 20, 111.
207. Chaudhuri, *Autobiography*, loc. 14038-14047.
208. Rear-Admiral Viscount Mountbatten of Burma's personal report no 17, dated 16 August 1947.
209. Ibid.
210. Pamela Mountbatten, *India Remembered*, pp 74, 118.
211. Pothen, *Glittering Decades*, loc. 2191-2202.
212. Pothen, *Glittering Decades*, loc. 2250.
213. Mountbatten, *India Remembered*, p 197.
214. Chaudhuri, *Autobiography*, loc. 14845-14854; Lal, *Dilli mein das varsh*, pp 64-5; Pothen, *Glittering Decades*, loc. 2458.
215. Mountabtten, *India Remembered*, p 234.
216. Lal, *Dilli mein das varsh*, pp 72-5.
217. Ibid., p 6; Pothen, *Glittering Decades*, loc.2527, 2458, 2631.
218. Lal, *Dilli mein das varsh*, pp 78, 111-13; Pothen, *Glittering Decades*, loc. 2631.
219. Nevile, *Carefree Days*, loc 883.
220. Sengupta, *Delhi Metropolitan*, p 88.
221. Sengupta, *Delhi Metropolitan*, p 230.
222. Sengupta, *Delhi Metropolitan*, pp 198, 203; Map in Delhi State Archives: 'Plan showing all the temporary buildings in New Delhi erected in connection with the war'.

223. Singh, *Perpetual City*, p 72; Sengupta, *Delhi Metropolitan*, p 223; Lalit Nirula, 'Growing up in CP'.
224. Ravinder Kaur, 'Claiming community through narratives: Punjabi refugees in Delhi' in Romi Khosla, ed., *The Idea of Delhi*, Marg Publications, New Delhi, 2005, p 65.
225. Note by Swinton on the layout of New Delhi, dated 19 December 1912. Hasan and Patel, eds., *From Ghalib's Dilli to Lutyens' New Delhi*, p 65.

Image credits

Private collection: *Facing i, 1, 3, 8, 10, 15, 22, 27, 32, 36, 86, 101, 103, 105*

Illustration by Neeti Banerji: *23, 24*

Universal History Archive/UIG via Getty images: *30 (Portrait of Edwin Lutyens)*

Wikimedia: *30 (Portrait of Herbert Baker)*

Delhi State Archives: *41, 43, 64, 68, 73, 76*

Photo Division, Ministry of Information and Broadcasting: *Cover, 48, 55, 81, 89, 96, 99, 106, 111, 134, 137, 139*

Jayshree Shukla: *61, 145*

Swapna Liddle: *113, 120, 150, 153, 156*

Sondeep Shankar: *124, 141*

Nehru Memorial Museum and Library: *130*

Gopalan Rajamani: *152*

ALSO BY SWAPNA LIDDLE IN SPEAKING TIGER

Chandni Chowk
The Mughal City of Old Delhi

'A wonderful and much-needed introduction to the history of the Old City of Delhi and a welcome addition to the literature on Shahjahanabad.'
—William Dalrymple

What we know today as Chandni Chowk was once a part of one of the greatest cities of the world—the imperial city established by the Mughal emperor Shahjahan in the seventeenth century, and named after him—Shahjahanabad. This is the story of how the city came to be established, its grandeur as the capital of an empire at its peak, and its important role in shaping the language and culture of North India. It is also the story of the many tribulations the city has seen—the invasion of Nadir Shah, the Revolt of 1857, Partition.

Today, Shahjahanabad has been subsumed under the gigantic sprawl of metropolitan Delhi. Yet it has an identity that is distinct. Popularly known as Chandni Chowk, its name conjures up romantic narrow streets, a variety of street food and exotic markets. For Shahjahanabad is still very much a living city, though the lives of the people inhabiting it have changed over the centuries. Dariba Kalan still has rows of flourishing jewellers' shops; Begum Samru's haveli is now Bhagirath Palace, a sprawling electronics market, and no visit to Chandni Chowk is complete without a meal at Karim's, whose chefs use recipes handed down to them through the ages for their mouth-watering biriyani and kebabs.

Swapna Liddle draws upon a wide variety of sources, such as the accounts of Mughal court chroniclers, travellers' memoirs, poetry, newspapers and government documents, to paint a vivid and dynamic panorama of the city from its inception to recent times.

PAGE EXTENT: 196PP; PRICE: RS 399

www.ingramcontent.com/pod-product-compliance
Lightning Source LLC
Chambersburg PA
CBHW051118230426
43667CB00014B/2632